Rogs P
B/DF
AF469568

WOLVERHAMPTON WANDERERS GREATS

WOLVERHAMPTON WANDERERS GREATS

David Instone

Foreword by
Graham Turner

SPORTSPRINT PUBLISHING
EDINBURGH

Dedication

To those players who made Wolverhampton Wanderers great, to those I hope will make them great again in future and to the fans whose dedication and loyalty never cease to amaze me.

© David Instone 1990

All rights reserved.
No part of this publication may be reproduced in any form or by any means without the prior permission of the publishers,
John Donald Publishers Ltd.,
138 St Stephen Street, Edinburgh EH3 5AA

ISBN 0 85976 312 9

British Library Cataloguing in Publication Data
Instone, David
Wolverhampton Wanderers Greats.
1. England. Association football. Biographies. Collections
I. Title
796.3340922

Phototypeset by Beecee Typesetting Services
Printed in Great Britain by Bell & Bain Ltd., Glasgow

Foreword

I'm sure it's impossible to spend any time watching, supporting or working for Wolverhampton Wanderers, without becoming aware of the club's magnificent traditions.

I grew up at a time when Wolves were the Liverpool of the Football League and consider myself fortunate to have supported them, albeit from a distance. The fans who populated Molineux in the 1950s, especially, were very lucky people.

The famous names roll off the tongue like a who's who of some of English football's greatest players. Not just those whose careers are highlighted in detail in David Instone's appreciation of his ten best post-war Wolves players, but also those who could claim to have just missed inclusion. In this club's case, you could have compiled a list of 50 post-war greats and still had many players left over whom other clubs would have been queueing up for.

To a man, the ten selected players have absolutely phenomenal records. They are or were players any manager would gladly have or have had in his squad. It's no wonder Wolves have had that undoubted knack of putting trophies in the cabinet over the years.

For my own part, I take great pride in seeing the name of one of today's stars, Steve Bull, included in the line-up. I would love to think that if the book is updated at the end of the century or re-written along similar lines, there would be two or three 1990s Wolves players in the top ten.

The club's glorious past is an incentive to us all to see the great days return. I am delighted that we have brought some success back to Molineux in recent years and nothing would thrill me more than to see us go on to emulate some of the wonderful deeds achieved by Billy Wright, Stan Cullis and the rest.

Graham Turner

Acknowledgements

I am greatly indebted to friends, associates and players, too numerous to mention individually, for the supply of many excellent illustrations.

I am particularly grateful to the *Express & Star* for their generous loan of photographs used in this publication.

D.I.

Contents

CHAPTER 1

Introduction

IT WAS AT BOURNEMOUTH ON A SPRING EVENING a few months ago that I first challenged a friend of mine to name the ten players he considered the best in Wolverhampton Wanderers' post-war history.

He didn't take much prompting to reel off the first few 'Bully, of course,' he said, 'John Richards, Mike Bailey, Dave Wagstaffe. Oh, and Kenny Hibbitt, definitely. Maybe Derek Parkin as well.' At that point, I interrupted and explained that the choice should be made on the last 45 years, not just the last 20.

He then turned the tables and asked, having been told I was writing a book on the subject, who I had selected. I recited my list and received a less-than-enthusiastic reception.

I went on to say I had spent a few hours in the company of Stan Cullis that very morning and that he had applauded my choice of 'stars'. Or nine of them, at least, He was much too modest to accept that he, having played a few games after the war, had a right to be in there as well.

'What does Stan Cullis know about it?' my friend continued, at which point I thought it was time to terminate the conversation. Then a broad smile spread across his face and he assured me he knew full well why Cullis was one of the most famous names in Wolves' history.

He even started to accept that there was a place in the list for Billy Wright, Johnny Hancocks, Jimmy Mullen — players he had only read about and had been told about. But the point was that he had his favourites — men who belonged to the era he had grown up in. And that's the case with virtually every football fan the length and breadth of the country.

As well as informing and, to a degree, educating on Wolves' glorious history, I hope this book will serve as a stimulus to supporters to think about who THEY think are the best ten players to have pulled on the famous gold and black since the war.

Many older fans will no doubt wonder why Dennis Westcott is not there, or perhaps Jesse Pye. And they will ask how Bill Shorthouse, Roy Pritchard, Jimmy Murray and Eddie Clamp could possibly be left out. Roy Swinbourne will have his supporters, too, while Dennis Wilshaw scored goals in such abundance as to impress the fiercest critic.

More recently, Hibbitt, Bailey and Wagstaffe have been firm crowd favourites. And Derek Dougan was the darling of the North Bank for several years in the late 1960s and early 1970s. On long service alone, you have to consider the merits of Geoff Palmer and Parkin, the latter having played more games for the club than anyone else living or dead.

It might have been easier to select a top 20 Wolves greats, then Eddie Stuart, Malcolm Finlayson, George Showell and Sammy Smyth could have been guaranteed places. But a whole host of other players would have become borderline cases, which would have set the ball rolling all over again.

It was impossible to write this book without having somebody doubting my judgement. I, too, was brought up in an era of Flowerses, Dougans, Richardses and Wagstaffes and have had to look and learn to establish the true greatness of the men who preceded them.

In the course of that enlightening search, I have visited and interviewed players from London to Oakengates — and offer a big thank-you for their time, their hospitality and their coffee and biscuits. But thanks most of all to them for serving up some wonderful memories and offering an insight to those who missed their heyday.

CHAPTER 2

Stan Cullis

TO THE MODERN WULFRUNIAN — THE NAME FOR the native of Wolverhampton — the Merseyside town of Ellesmere Port may not seem particularly significant. A smallish dot a few degrees off an imaginary straight line between Chester and Birkenhead on the map and a 13-letter name appearing between the Norfolk village of Ellingham and the Shropshire version of Ellesmere in the accompanying index.

But to the educated fan of Wolverhampton Wanderers, it is one of the most important breeding grounds in England. A breeding ground, that is, for two men who have played huge parts in the post-war history of one of Europe's most famous football clubs.

Graham Turner, the manager who has steered Wolves from the Fourth Division to the top half of the Second and taken them to Wembley twice in the process, was born there in October, 1947.

A few houses away in the very same street, almost exactly 31 years earlier, one Stanley Cullis made his first appearance in this world. And the day in 1934 when he moved the 70 or so miles to Wolverhampton proved to be one of the most important in Wolves' long and distinguished history.

By the time he walked out of the Molineux doors for the last time as an employee in 1964, Cullis had helped the club win the League championship three times and the F.A. Cup twice. There was also the small matter of being beaten F.A. Cup finalists in 1938/39, of being First Division runners-up five times and of finishing elsewhere in the top six a further nine times. In short, Cullis inspired them to become the Liverpool of the late 1940s and the 1950s. No one man, from Noel George and Tom Phillipson to Turner and Steve Bull, has done more to make sure the name of Wolverhampton Wanderers is remembered and revered forever.

Cullis considers himself lucky to have been involved in Wolves' glory years and Wolves should certainly never forget their good fortune in accounting for 30 years of Cullis's working life. But the marriage between the two was more than mere accident.

Early in the 20th century, hundreds of working people left Wolverhampton with the town's Corrugated Iron Company and moved north-west to Ellesmere Port. Included in the exodus were proud parents William and Elizabeth Cullis.

Ellesmere became fondly known among the new arrivals as 'Little Wolverhampton' and the ties with the parent town were by no means severed. Especially in the Cullis household.

The young Stanley was soon attracting the Football League scouts as he banged in the goals as a promising inside-forward with both the Cambridge Road school team and the Ellesmere schoolboys' side. Bolton Wanderers gave him a trial in 1933 but Mr Cullis Snr had the future neatly mapped out. 'If I consider my boy is good enough, he will join Wolverhampton Wanderers,' he said. Well, he was and he did, although fans of Everton and Liverpool were never slow in later years to remind him they didn't greatly appreciate his decision to turn his back on Merseyside!

Ellesmere-based Football League referee Joe Forshaw took the step of recommending Master Cullis to then Wolves manager Major Frank Buckley and, without anything as trivial as a trial, a contract was signed.

'The Major certainly ensured I kept my feet on the

On to the hallowed turf . . . Cullis leads Billy Wright and the rest of his players out before their 3-1 victory over Leicester City at Wembley in 1949. Pictured following Wright are Roy Pritchard and Bill Shorthouse.

ground,' Cullis recalls. 'My first weekly wage was two pounds ten shillings, with five shillings win bonus, and I was called back from Ellesmere Port in the middle of my first summer to weed the Molineux pitch and lay some new seed!

'I was living with my aunt in Wolverhampton and my early grooming at Molineux made sure there wasn't much chance of me becoming full of my own importance.'

Cullis, by this time converted to a wing-half (something like a defensive midfielder in 1990s terminology), was obvious captaincy material and soon heard the words that put an extra spring in his youthful step. 'The Major called me into his office and said: "Cullis, I will make you skipper of Wolves one day." But his statement carried the important rider: "If you listen and do what you are told!" Nevertheless, it was a big boost to me so early in my career.

'Whatever I was involved in, I always seemed to end up as

captain, whether it was cricket and football at school or if I'd decided to take up tennis and golf for that matter. Some people don't relish the responsibility but it didn't bother me at all. In fact I liked it, even when Sir Stanley Rous reminded me when I was England captain that I was responsible not only for my own actions on the field but also those of my team-mates!'

Cullis's rise to prominence was truly extraordinary. He captained the Wolves third team at 17, their reserves at 18, their first team at 19 and was made official club captain in the week of his 20th birthday. As if that wasn't enough, he skippered the Football League against the Scottish League at 21 and, after turning 22, took the inevitable step of being made one of England's youngest-ever captains.

As a little-known teenager, though, promises of the club captaincy or not, the man who was to make Wolves great more than a decade later had actually threatened to turn his back on Molineux before the ink was dry on the first chapter of the fairytale. William Cullis, on hearing his son had not been given a wage rise after his first season, immediately sent him a 'Refuse terms, come home' telegram. Fortunately, not least for Wolves, the Major relented and put another ten shillings in the youngster's pay packet. It was one of the best day's work Buckley ever did at Molineux and probably avoided the worst possible example of false economy!

So, Cullis continued to make his mark in the Wolves A team in the Birmingham Combination. But, as so often happens, it was a lucky break which provided the first steps towards stardom.

Buckley, believing his side to be short of attacking power, signed Irishman Dave 'Boy' Martin and then found that injury had robbed him of a centre-half to mark him in a first team v reserves practice match one Tuesday morning. Cullis was still playing as a wing-half but, at the suggestion of trainer Jack Davies, was switched in emergency to the No. 5 position. Martin hardly had a kick and Cullis hardly had another game anywhere but at centre-half. It was the turning point of his playing career.

Football fashion, pre-war style . . . Stan Cullis the player lines up for the 1938-39 Wolves. Back row from left: Billy Morris, Tom Galley, Alec Scott, Frank Taylor, Joe Gardiner. Front: Jimmy Mullen, 'Dizzy' Burton, Alec McIntosh, Stan Cullis, Dennis Westcott, Dicky Dorsett, Ted Maguire.

He was called up for first-team duty in the game against Huddersfield shortly afterwards and soon became an established and accomplished First Division defender, reeling off 38 appearances the following season and 46 in 1938/39. The next logical step, with experience already acquired in the Football League side, was elevation to the full England side — an honour which came Cullis's way on October 23, 1937, two days before his 21st birthday. England's opponents were Northern Ireland in Belfast and a 5-1 victory made it a pleasing start for the Wolves man, especially as he did a good marking job on Dave 'Boy' Martin, the forward who by this time had moved on to Nottingham Forest.

Cullis retained his place for the match against Wales at Middlesbrough a month later, when he lined up for the first time alongside the legendary Stanley Matthews, and collected further caps in the home games against Czechoslovakia at Tottenham and Scotland at Wembley.

After a brief absence, he again became a regular in 1938-39 and says: 'Representing England was the highlight of my playing career. I've always considered playing for your country to be the highest accolade you can receive. But the war came along at a time when I was becoming established and my last full cap was against Rumania in Bucharest in May, 1939. Although I played in 20 or so wartime games for England, they didn't count as full caps and I lost my place to Neil Franklin after the war.'

Cullis, by this time earning something approaching £8 a week at Wolves, plus £2 for a win and a further £8 a game when he represented England, seemed set for an F.A. Cup winner's medal at the end of 1938-39. First Division runners-up Wolves had battled through to the Wembley final for the first time in 18 years and opponents Portsmouth, from the wrong end of the First Division, were seen as little more than cannon fodder. But, against all the odds, Pompey ran out 4-1 winners.

It soon became clear that Cullis and his colleagues wouldn't even be able to console themselves with the age-old saying 'There's always next year.' By the time next year came around, Hitler was on the march through Europe, so League football was suspended for more than six years.

Cullis, who had expected the worst and joined the South Staffords six months earlier in anticipation of hostilities breaking out, spent what should have been the peak years of his playing career working as a physical training instructor. He was posted to Bari in southern Italy for a while and had to contend himself with organising matches for the troops.

But, if he is expected to wallow in self-pity at the international caps and the hundreds of extra League and Cup appearances that got away, he has some poignant words: 'Not for one moment did I bemoan what I might have lost. I came home from the war in one piece and that was something to be grateful for. We all know that a lot of young men weren't so lucky.'

The England side's foray into Europe earned Cullis, now undoubtedly a top-class centre-half — outstanding in the air, strong and solid on the ground — admirers the world over. But he also made a few enemies with the determined streak and intelligence that went hand in hand with his playing ability.

As an 18-year-old, he had clashed with a Wolves director over tactics in a reserve game at Blackpool and, as a seasoned international some years later, he incurred the wrath of sections of the country's Press following an England wartime game against Wales.

'As captain, I had quite a big say in tactics then because there was no manager — just selectors. I heard before the game that Wales were going to put two men on Stanley Matthews. As a result, I decided we would attack on the left through Dennis Compton instead of on the right through Stan. We won five or six but the newspapers gave me a right rollicking and asked how I'd dared treat Stanley Matthews like that. They insisted the spectators had gone to watch Matthews, not me, and demanded that I be forced to give up the captaincy. Then I had a letter from Stanley Rous at the FA and was reassured: "You will remain as captain." It was nice to know I had the backing of the people who really mattered.'

It was during the war that Cullis suffered the first in the series of concussion injuries that were to bring his playing career to a close. He was hit on the chin in an army fixture and spent a fortnight in hospital. He also spent seven days under strict observation after a collision in a game at Everton and, when he had to be rushed to hospital in Sheffield during a train journey home from a post-war Wolves game at Middlesbrough, he knew it was time to think about hanging up his boots.

But he decided to play for one more season — 1946-47 — by which time former Bolton Wanderers and Wales winger Ted Vizard had replaced Buckley as manager. Cullis had been tempted by a move to Hull City, complete with the promise of a house, but Wolves' directors had come up with an attractive offer of their own — the chance for him to become assistant to Vizard in the summer of 1947. Cullis took up the latter option and spent another nine eventful months in the famous old gold.

Wolves, inspired by the goals of Dennis Westcott, led the table at one stage by an incredible 11 points but were held up by the snow and ice and went five weeks without a game. Following the thaw, they lost their way and came to their last game on May 31 with the title hanging delicately in the balance.

Victory or even, possibly, a draw at a packed Molineux would give Wolves the championship. But opponents Liverpool could pip them to English football's top prize if they won. And it was the Merseysiders who came out on top 2-1 in a gripping struggle.

'Albert Stubbins scored one of Liverpool's goals after he got the wrong side of me and set off towards goal,' Cullis said. 'A lot of people have since asked me why I didn't bring him down or pull him back by his shirt — and I suppose I could have done. But I didn't want to go down in history as the man who decided the destiny of a championship with a professional foul.'

So, Wolves eventually finished behind Liverpool and Manchester United and Cullis, whose retirement at 31 had been announced to a hushed crowd just before kick-off, retreated into the role of running the club's reserves and being dispatched to watch would-be new signings and so continue an excellent talent-spotting policy introduced by Major Buckley.

But Cullis wasn't to be out of the limelight for long, Vizard resigning at the end of the 1947-48 season, in which Wolves finished fifth in the First Division and suffered an early F.A. Cup exit at the hands of Everton. Cullis was the ready-made replacement and stepped up into the hot seat for the following season.

He was a popular choice and the directors' judgement was to prove spot-on. Cullis's 16 years in charge were the most successful period in the club's history and Wolves became the talk of the football world. The first major post-war trophy was to follow only a few months later with a 3-1 win over Leicester City in the Wembley final of the F.A. Cup. They reached the fifth round before losing in a replay to Blackpool in 1949-50 and lost in the semi-final to Newcastle United in 1950-51.

But Wolves were still a force in the League as well,

Nearing the end . . . Cullis again in the captain's position, ball at his feet, this time in 1946-47. Back row from left: Ted Vizard (manager), Tom Galley, Angus McLean, Bert Williams, Billy Crook, Billy Wright, Jack Smith (trainer), Jack Howley (secretary). Front: Johnny Hancocks, Jesse Pye, Dennis Westcott, Stan Cullis, Willie Forbes, Jimmy Mullen.

finishing sixth and second in Cullis's first two years and then bouncing back from two poor seasons (14th and 16th) to come third in 1952-53. 'Most people thought the team I was lucky enough to play in just before the war was the best Wolves had ever produced,' he added. 'But I would say the post-war side was better.'

Wartime was becoming a fading memory by the time Wolves confirmed they had reached the pinnacle of the domestic game by carrying off the title in 1953-54. Neighbours Albion pushed them all the way but fell by the wayside as Billy Wright picked up the championship trophy instead. And there was nearly a repeat in 1954-55, Wolves being pipped into second place in a season in which they also reached the Cup quarter-finals.

Molineux was alight with wonderful players and

achievements and was to remain awash with fantastic memories for decades afterwards. It wasn't only the names adorning the other chapters in this book that brought glory to the club. There were also the slightly lesser names — Bill Shorthouse, Roy Swinbourne, George Showell, Eddie Stuart, Roy Pritchard, Eddie Clamp, Sammy Smyth, Norman Deeley, Dennis Wilshaw, Jimmy Murray, Bobby Mason, Nigel Sims, Jesse Pye, Ray Chatham, John Short, Billy Crook, Jimmy Dunn, Angus McLean, Terry Springthorpe, Lol Kelly, Tom Galley, Leslie Smith and Colin Booth among them.

Wolves were third again in 1955-56, sixth in 1956-57 and champions both in 1957-58 and 1958-59 — becoming only the ninth club ever to successfully defend the championship.

The Molineux trophy cabinet was hardly big enough to cope with all the spoils of Wolves' success but, away from the League championships and the F.A. Cup successes, the club was achieving something more momentous. 'It was very nice to win the cups and the League but, for sheer excitement, they were some way behind my fondest memories,' Cullis added. 'The floodlit matches we staged in the mid-1950s were even better. There was nothing to compare to them. They were the high spot of Wolves' entire history.

'The games against Honved, Moscow Spartak, Real Madrid and Moscow Dynamo were something that will stay in my mind for ever. They were fantastic matches and fantastic occasions. The very fact that they were played under lights made them special because we were pioneers of floodlit football. I remember the chairman asking me once if I thought we should have lights installed out of the profits we made every year. Villa and Albion were thinking along the same lines but we were bold enough to go ahead with the idea while they seemed to sit back to see whether our experiment with them was a success.

'To say that the experiment was a booming success would be an understatement. Suddenly, we were playing some of the world's top sides at Molineux and the fans loved it. It didn't matter for one moment that the matches were only friendlies. We changed to fluorescent gold shirts because they showed up better in the dark and I became quite adept at speech-making what with all the banquets we had after the games!'

With the likes of Malcolm Finlayson, Gerry Harris, Harry Hooper, Des Horne and Barry Stobart emerging in the late 1950s, it was a case of Wembley revisited in 1959-60. Wolves, pipped by Burnley while seeking to complete a hat-trick of title successes, suffered no such disappointment along a Cup trail that ended with a 3-0 victory over Blackburn Rovers.

Cullis had more than made up for surprisingly missing out as a player 21 years earlier and says: 'Going to Wembley as a manager and winning the F.A. Cup, you have to consider yourself one of the luckiest men alive. Just being involved in a final is sufficient really but going home in triumph is tremendous. I remember the Press photographers wanted me to do a lap of honour afterwards but I refused. I didn't want to take any limelight away from the players. And when the cameramen asked for a picture of me drinking champagne in the dressing-room, I had to say no again. I didn't drink. I offered to pose drinking a cup of tea but they weren't very impressed. They said their sports editors would have gone mad at seeing a Cup-winning manager drinking tea!'

Wolves followed up by finishing third in 1960-61 and that, sadly, was the end of the Cullis golden era. He stayed as manager for another three and a bit years, during which the club finished 18th, 5th and 16th, but the old magic had gone. So had the really great players, although Peter Broadbent and Ron Flowers were to stay a while longer. On September 15, 1964, with Wolves already locked in a survival battle that was to end in defeat, came the announcement that Cullis had been sacked.

Just recovered from illness, he had given the club more than 30 years of his working life and Molineux was in turmoil for months afterwards. Some fans never forgave the directors for their actions but Andy Beattie was installed as manager and a new era had begun. It seemed typical of this black relegation season that one of Cullis's mentors, Major Frank Buckley, died in mid-winter.

As well as the two F.A. Cup successes and the trio of Football League championship triumphs, Cullis had steered Wolves to glory in the Charity Shield, the F.A. Youth Cup and the Central League. He had made them the club to beat in the country that gave football to the world — and he was assured of a place in Molineux folklore. But what was the secret of his success?

In his 1959 autobiography, *All For The Wolves*, he wrote: 'My war-time experiences in the army taught me that proper training can cause the abnormal achievement to become the normal one. Thus, the man who couldn't walk a mile with a shopping basket was often marching ten miles at a smart pace with a hefty load on his back by 1943.' And, now in his mid seventies, he insisted to me at his home in the shadow of the Malvern Hills that physical fitness was very much a key to Wolves' success.

'People used to say I was an iron-man as a manager. But I had a principle that the players were representing the town of Wolverhampton as well as just Wolverhampton Wanderers. It was their duty to acknowledge that and, for that reason, they had to work hard. I'm sure our training schedule was as hard as anybody's in the country but it paid off. Very often, we would win matches in the last ten or 15 minutes.

'Frank Morris, a three A's runner, was responsible for the stamina side of the training and the players were certainly put through it. But I never swore at them and I didn't expect them to swear at me.

'Our tactics were fairly simple. I don't think the Wolves crowd wanted or expected too many frills. They were just keen that we scored at least one more goal than the opposition! I insisted we should be direct, getting the ball upfield as soon as possible. I wanted us to play at a pace that was too much for the other team.'

And that, in the clearest possible terms, is the message with which Cullis sent his players out to perform their magic. The man who grew up in the same boys' teams as Joe Mercer and later modelled himself on Matt Busby, himself became a model for those who followed him in British and European football. Wolverhampton Wanderers, clearly, would never have been the same without him.

FULL INTERNATIONAL CAPS (12)

(England score given first)

1937: Northern Ireland (Belfast) 5-1; Wales (Middlesbrough) 2-1; Czechoslovakia (Tottenham) 5-4.

1938: Scotland (Wembley) 0-1; France (Paris) 4-2; FIFA (Arsenal) 3-0; Norway (Newcastle) 4-0; Northern Ireland (Manchester) 7-0.

1939: Scotland (Hampden) 2-1; Italy (Milan) 2-2; Yugoslavia (Belgrade) 1-2; Rumania (Bucharest) 2-0.

WOLVES APPEARANCES

League: 152. F.A. Cup: 19. Total: 171. Goals 0.

CHAPTER 3

Billy Wright

WHEN SIR JACK HAYWARD COMPLETED HIS big-money takeover of Wolverhampton Wanderers at the end of the 1989-90 season, he quickly spelled out one of his dearest wishes: that the club of his dreams would once again return to producing their own stars.

As an example, he talked of a small blond-haired boy from Ironbridge, who made the short move to Molineux after finishing school in the 1930s and went on to travel and thrill the world, winning 105 England caps and playing in 490 Football League matches. As Sir Jack spoke, the same small, blond lad stood at his side — now a distinguished 66-year-old newcomer to the Wolves board. His name: William Ambrose Wright CBE.

If Wolves were the kings of English football in the 1950s, as indeed they were, then Wright was the jewel in their crown. The greatest among greats. And his story is one that should act as an inspiration to the current generation of small boys, from whose masses Sir Jack Hayward hopes to see a gem or two unearthed.

Wright was once discarded from Molineux because he wasn't big enough. But, thankfully, then manager Major Frank Buckley saw the error of his ways and took him back. It's one of sport's all-time understatements to say the decision to rethink was a wise one. Much of the excellent talent-spotting

That winning feeling . . . Wolves players (from left) Jimmy Dunn, Bert Williams, Bill Shorthouse, Jesse Pye, Terry Springthorpe, Jimmy Mullen and Roy Pritchard make sure Billy Wright has an easy ride round Wembley after the side's 3-1 victory over Leicester City.

Buckley did would have been undone had he let pass through his fingers a lad who was to grow up into one of the world's finest-ever footballers.

Wright went on to skipper his club and country more times than he cares to remember, to enter the elite band of players to have appeared in the final stages of three World Cups and to inspire his team to one F.A. Cup triumph and three League championship successes. Perhaps even more notable than that, though, he was a magnificent ambassador and a true gentleman on and off the field. A man who played hard but never forgot that the spirit in which a match was played was more important than whether it was won or lost. At a time when football helped rebuild bridges of friendship around the world, Billy Wright played as big a part as anybody.

So what of those crucial early days, when Wolves discovered and then nearly squandered a player who, at his peak, would have been worth millions in today's market? Wright was born in Ironbridge, Shropshire, on February 6, 1924, the son of an iron founder and a Coalport china designer. He had a liking for Arsenal as a boy and, in his days at Madeley Senior School, showed promise as a centre-forward, once scoring ten goals in a game!

But it was with Wolves, courtesy of an advert in a local paper, that he made his name — as a wing-half and centre-half. He signed at Molineux in 1938, the Major putting him on 40 shillings a week and telling him that, if he was to make it, he would both have to learn to run properly and to grow.

Wright moved in with fellow hopeful Alan Steen at the Tettenhall home of Mr and Mrs Arthur Colley, who lived a twopenny bus ride from Molineux. His lodgings accounted for 30 of the 40 shillings that appeared weekly in his pay packet but, more significantly, he had found the stable background from which he was to blossom.

Wright, nicknamed 'Snowy' by Tom Galley when he was introduced several days later to the first-teamers, was utterly dedicated. He didn't drink or smoke and what time he had available outside football was filled with homely pursuits like reading Dickens, listening to classical music and even embroidering tablecloths! He made his first appearance for the club in a B match against Walsall Wood in the Walsall Minor League and he was still only 14 years and three months — and on an eight-month trial — when he received the news which could have changed his life.

'Major Buckley called me in and I looked at him, dressed in his brown tweed suit and with his piercing eyes behind thick horn-rimmed glasses,' Wright recalled. 'He said: "I'm afraid you haven't grown up to be a professional footballer, sonny. There's nothing else for it. You'll have to return home." Even before I had closed the door on the manager's office, I could feel tears beginning to well up. Without realising I was crying, Alan Steen rested one hand on my shoulder and said: "Don't take any notice. He'll change his mind in another five minutes".'

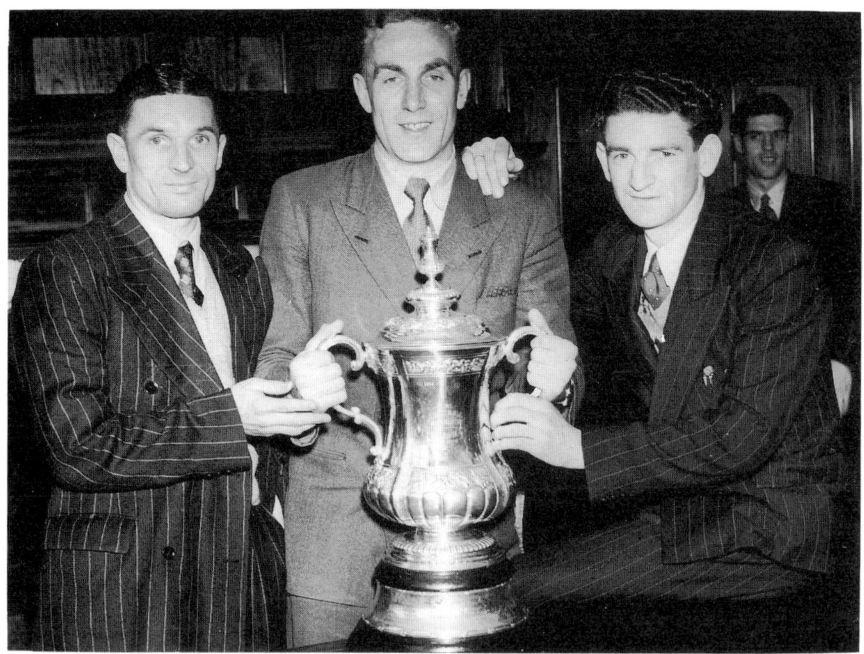

Happy threesome . . . Johnny Hancocks, Billy Wright and Roy Pritchard with the spoils of Wolves' 1948-49 season — the F.A. Cup. In the background is Laurie Kelly.

It took a little longer than five minutes but, after the broken-hearted teenager had chosen the privacy of the referee's room in which to weep, the Major did change his mind. Groundsman Albert Tye broke the good news of the rethink, which he, trainer Jack Davies and secretary Jack Howley had helped bring about by saying how good young Billy was — as a sweeper-out of the dressing room! The added intervention of Mr and Mrs Colley in getting their lodger fixed up with a £3-a-week job at the Goodyear tyre company was further encouragement. The story that was to turn into a fairytale was resumed.

Wright proceeded to work his way through the club's junior sides and knew he was heading in the right direction when he was selected to pack the skip as the first team set off for their F.A. Cup final date with Portsmouth at Wembley in 1939! But it was after the outbreak of war that he made his senior debut in a 2-1 win at Notts County.

His career progressed rapidly from there. He turned professional at 17, receiving the £10 signing-on fee that came with it, and turned out alongside Jimmy Mullen as a guest for Leicester City when the worsening of the hostilities prompted Wolves to suspend playing competitive football. With Wright switching between outside right, centre-half and the two wing-half positions, the duo totalled 23 goals between them in one season, including one apiece in a 2-0 win against Walsall in a Midland Youth Cup final victory.

But he suffered another setback when he fractured his ankle in a War Cup semi-final against West Bromwich Albion at Molineux and was out for three months. It could have been a lot worse, though, for there were brief fears that his career was over.

As it turned out, he recovered in good time to sign up for military service at 18 and was disappointed at not joining the Navy. Instead, he did a PT course and then became a corporal in the General Services Corps at Copthorne Barracks, Shrewsbury. In two years, he played only a few games for Wolves but still stood out — by now as a fine young inside-left. He scored a hat-trick in 17 minutes in one game against Nottingham Forest and fans wrote to Molineux telling Buckley that that proved he was a forward, not a defender!

Football was still in disarray as a result of the war but, while full internationals and the League programme were suspended, there were still stages for the country's best to display their talents on. Wright earned representative honours for Western Command before being posted to the Army Physical Training School at Aldershot and it was while down South in August, 1945 that he was selected for the first time for international duty.

The nature of the call-up was certainly unusual, with Corporal Wright of the Shropshire Light Infantry hard at work in a lecture room when Regimental Sergeant Major Dennis entered. He handed him a white card telling him he was CB. Wright feared he had been guilty of some misdemeanour and

Typically Wright . . . Immaculate timing makes up for the lack of inches as this Leicester attack is ended in the 1949 F.A. Cup final.

started to worry about being court-martialled. Little did he know that CB, for the purpose of the surprise, actually stood for cap-bound!

Wright's call-up was as reserve for an F.A. trip to Ireland, where, on arrival in Belfast, the streets were packed by thousands waving Union Jacks. The new boy inquired of team-mate Neil Franklin as to whether the huge turn-out was in the team's honour. It was only when they reached their hotel and a massive cheer broke out that everything fell into place. Field Marshal Viscount Montgomery was arriving at the same time to be granted the Freedom of the City!

Wright was an eager spectator at the F.A. side's 1-0 victory but was sadly out of form when given his chance in the Combined Services XI team that lost 1-0 to the Irish League on the same trip. He was sharing a room with Franklin and was in despondent mood as he switched off the light that night. 'After that, I don't suppose I stand a chance of winning a full international cap,' he said. To which Franklin replied: 'Don't worry, things will work out. You've started so young, you might even break the cap record.'

It was an astonishing statement, no matter how tongue-in-cheek, but Wright was so determined to make the big time that anything was possible. In 1946, he stated his intentions by declining a trial with Worcestershire County Cricket Club and, with the League still not resumed, his international career seemed to be progressing faster than his club career.

The F.A. selected him again for the victory internationals against Belgium at home and Scotland at Hampden Park, the thrill of his first trip to Wembley being heightened when he was also asked to sign his first autograph! Wright was down to play again at inside-left but Frank Soo pulled out at short notice, so he switched to right-half, with Wolves team-mate Jesse Pye coming in at No. 10.

His first F.A. game outside the British Isles took him to Paris for a bruising 2-0 defeat against the French and, by the time he turned out again for the unofficial national side four months later — against Scotland at Manchester City's ground — soccer and life were returning to normal. The Football League restarted in 1946-47 and international appearances again brought full caps.

The first of his staggering collection of 105 caps came in the Wilf Mannion-inspired slaughter of Ireland in Belfast on September 28, 1946, and another 32 England games and four years nine days were to pass before he missed a senior England

Just beautiful . . . Wright with Cup, 1949. *Picture courtesy of Topical.*

game. Wright was to play in such memorable matches as the 8-2 crushing of Holland at Huddersfield in late 1946, the 5-2 win over Belgium in Brussels in 1947 and, in between, the 10-0 Lisbon romp over a Portuguese side bombarded with cushions by their fans and then shamed by their performance into staying away from the post-match banquet!

During Wright's same run of 33 successive appearances,

England also beat Sweden 4-2 at Arsenal, Switzerland 6-0 at the same venue and Northern Ireland 9-2 at Manchester City. But life was good at Molineux, too, with his League debut coming in Wolves' 6-1 victory over Arsenal on the first day of 1946-47. He was now on £5 a week at the club, with another £10 coming as bonus for Wolves' final placing of third.

On reporting back for duty two months later, the 23-year-old Wright was welcomed by manager Ted Vizard with the news: 'The directors have decided to make you skipper. Best of luck!' His appointment was followed by two steady seasons and he led the club to fifth and sixth respectively in 1947-48 and 1948-49, his inspirational value to the side obviously being closely monitored at F.A. headquarters.

And, in September, 1948, 14 months after being honoured with the Wolves captaincy, Wright heard the news that was to accelerate his blossoming career even further. While on his way home from England's goalless draw with the amateurs of Denmark in Copenhagen and clutching a giant ham he had brought home as a present, he boarded the bus taking him home to his digs. 'The conductress spotted me and passed on her congratulations,' he recalls. 'When I asked what for, she showed me a copy of the paper and pointed to an item in the Stop Press. There it was: I was to captain England against Ireland in Belfast a couple of weeks later. What a thrill! I couldn't believe it.

'There was criticism of my captaincy at various times in my career because I didn't believe in yelling at players on the field. But I knew there was nothing more likely to upset a team-mate than to be shown up in front of thousands of spectators. I preferred to lead by example and have a quiet word if necessary. The captain is the leader. He's the one who should never lose his composure because, if he does, he's likely to lose the respect of those around him.'

That low-key style was evident for the first time on the international stage when a 6-2 win in Belfast gave him a dream start as skipper. It was his 16th cap and the first of 90

Sporting greats . . . Wright and Hancocks meeting 1953 Derby winning jockey Sir Gordon Richards at a sportsmen's evening in Shropshire.

appearances as England captain. He switched to left-half for the game against Wales a month later and did likewise for two matches the following year. But right-half had become his England position.

At Wolves, where Stan Cullis — the finest player Wright ever played alongside or even saw — was now manager, he was mainly occupying the No. 6 shirt. And he savoured two of his finest ever games in 1948-49. 'Of all the matches I played for the club, I think my best and the one that really stands out was the F.A. Cup semi-final against Manchester United at Hillsborough,' he says. 'Roy Pritchard and Laurie Kelly were injured during the game and I went first to right-back and then to left-back to cover. Bert Williams was fantastic and we were delighted to get away with a 1-1 draw. In the replay in front of more than 72,000 at Goodison Park, Sammy Smyth scored the only goal and we were on the way to Wembley.

'We set off on the Thursday to prepare for the final and I asked Stan Cullis early in the journey what the team was going to be. After Lol Kelly, who had played at right-back for most of the season, found out he wasn't in, he got off the coach at Oxford. He was that upset and disappointed. It absolutely broke his heart. It was one of my worst jobs as captain to try to console him. Stan threatened him with all sorts of consequences but the matter was never mentioned again. I think the manager put himself in Lol's shoes when he calmed down and realised how he would have reacted.

'As for the big day itself, the Duke of Edinburgh and the Duke of Gloucester were introduced to the Wolves and Leicester players before kick-off. The Duke of Edinburgh had also met the England and Scotland players when I had been captain at Wembley three weeks earlier and he said as he shook my hand: "You must be getting to know this place by now!" They were great days. There were so many big matches.'

Wright was off on his England travels again that summer, this time on a tour of Sweden, Norway and France that brought him his first international goal — one of the three that set up his country's 3-1 win in Paris. Football still absolutely dominated his life. He was very much single but had developed a great love of music — a pursuit that led to an unusual encounter with an Italian journalist when the then World Cup holders took on England at Tottenham in the following November. The reporter heard of Wright's liking for gramophone records and, as promised, sent a consignment of them to his Tettenhall digs shortly afterwards!

That game brought Wright his second international goal — this time a freak cross-cum-shot which deceived keeper Moro — but he and his colleagues were less fortunate in the following summer's World Cup finals in Brazil. Rocked by the pre-tournament 'defection' of Neil Franklin, England suffered a shock defeat against the USA in Belo Horizonte — something akin to Germany beating the MCC at cricket, Wright said — and made an earlier-than-expected return home.

Wright's glittering career was taking one or two other wrong turns at about this time. A loss of form, an injury against Burnley and a failed driving test added to an unhappy sequence of events and Wolves sent him and winger Johnny Hancocks off to Blackpool for a month's recuperation, the duo returning only for matches. But the worry remained. In 1950-51, his performance in the 3-2 home defeat against Scotland was his worst yet for England and he flopped again in the follow-up Wembley triumph over Argentina. That was the end of his ever-present four-year run in the side, his place in the Festival of Britain match against Portugal ten days later going to Bill Nicholson, who rubbed salt into his rival's wounds by scoring with his first kick in international football.

There was now a gap of nearly five months before England's next game and Wright put the break to good effect. Previously unable to go on many of Wolves' close-season tours because of his international duties, he found a new challenge in his free summer of 1951 — and went with his club to South Africa. The trip certainly had the desired effect.

Wright regained his touch, came home refreshed and subsequently wrote in one of his autobiographies: 'Football again became a joy to me instead of a headache. The visit proved the turning point of my career. Freed from the strains of competitive football, I slowly but surely began to regain all the confidence I had been lacking.' And the first thing he said to his landlady on his return was: 'I want the season to open as quickly as possible, just to prove to everyone I'm not a has-been at 26.'

Wolves experienced a mediocre season but, sure enough, Wright was back in the England team as captain — not only for the 2-2 draw against France at Arsenal, but to stay! Incredibly, he didn't miss another England game until he retired 69 matches and nearly eight years later. He played in the win and the draw against the Austrian side then recognised as Europe's best team and, in the 3-0 win against Switzerland in Zurich on May 28, 1952, he passed Bob Crompton's record of 42 England caps.

Later in the same year, he also had his first taste of life as

England centre-half, taking over from the injured Jack Froggatt after half-an-hour of a game against Wales. In the 1954 World Cup finals, that was the position Wright was to make his own for many years to come.

Another honour was bestowed upon him when he was named Footballer of the Year in 1952 and cap No. 50 followed in Montevideo on another memorable end-of-season trip, this time to Argentina, Chile, Uruguay and North America in 1953. His half-century was marked by defeat against Uruguay but, in New York, there was revenge against a USA side containing Wright's former Wolves team-mate and fellow lodger, Terry Springthorpe.

England scored 18 goals in their next five matches, although the fourth match in the sequence was the infamous 6-3 Wembley defeat at the hands of Hungary in November, 1953. They were on the receiving end again in Budapest six months later in the shape of a 7-1 slaughter but there was good news in abundance for Wright closer to home.

The Molineux flame, which had been flickering with promise for some years, burned at its brightest in 1953-54. Floodlit football was about to take off and Wolves peaked at the right time as they headed off Albion's challenge to win the championship for the first time. 'There was nothing complicated about our strategy,' Wright says. 'It's just that we played attacking football and, if somebody scored against us, we went chasing goals at the other end with even greater vigour. There was hardly a dull moment. We conceded a fair few but we scored nearly a hundred ourselves!'

In that summer's World Cup finals in Switzerland, it was the same high-scoring story. England qualified comfortably from group four with a 4-4 draw against Belgium and a 2-0 win over the hosts but then lost 4-2 to holders Uruguay in the quarter-final.

Wright, switched to centre-half for the Swiss game in Berne, considers it the biggest disappointment of his career that, in an unprecedented three attempts as a World Cup

All in a day's work . . . Wright explaining how the championship was won in April, 1959.

captain, he couldn't lead England to anything like a successful campaign. After the side's knockout, though, he, team-mate Jimmy Dickinson and manager Walter Winterbottom stayed on to watch the rest of the competition, the Wolves skipper rating the Uruguay v Hungary semi-final in Lausanne as the best match he had ever seen.

Back at club level, Wright played 43 games in 1954-55 for

a side who finished First Division runners-up. Wolves' Cup hopes ended in the quarter-final at Sunderland, where the early loss of Bill Shorthouse through concussion provided a strong argument for the introduction of substitutes. Ten-man Wolves held out for another 80 minutes or so before finally cracking to two killer goals.

The 7-2 Wembley walloping of Scotland, to which Wolves forward Dennis Wilshaw contributed no fewer than four goals, was the highlight of the international season and Wright's caps tally stood at 68 after the unrewarding summer tour of France, Spain and Portugal.

With Wolves snapping away at the Football League's best in 1955-56, as well as dazzling more European visitors under the Molineux lights, Wright was still an outstanding force in the game, making up for his lack of inches with immaculate timing that enabled him to win both tackles on the ground and aerial battles with much bigger opponents. In addition, his speed and his remarkable anticipation quelled many dangerous situations before they even became apparent to others.

There was one particularly unhappy afternoon when Cullis switched him to left-back in an unsuccessful effort to stifle the 40-year-old Stanley Matthews, otherwise it was a magnificent march towards further glories — and records. In 1957-58, the League title returned to Molineux — the ground which had also provided the stage for Wright and his England colleagues to plunder a 5-2 victory over the Danes in the previous season.

But, for the second time, championship success didn't lead to World Cup glory for him because England — considered by some after their 5-0 November thrashing in Yugoslavia as being unfit to even go to the finals in Sweden — failed to progress beyond the group stage. With Wright flanked by Wolves team-mates Eddie Clamp and Bill Slater in three of the games — and Peter Broadbent making his international debut on the same trip — England drew with USSR, Brazil and Austria before losing in a play-off against the Russians.

The final curtain . . . With a tear and a hint of embarrassment, William Ambrose Wright acknowledges the guard of honour at his 1959 farewell. Also in picture are Eddie Stuart (his successor as captain), Malcolm Finlayson and Gerry Harris.

'It was one of those games against Russia,' Wright said. 'Their winning goal went in off the post and Peter Brabrook hit the post for us twice on his debut, only for the ball to bounce into the keeper's hands each time.'

There was one other big 'match' in his life in 1958 — his marriage to Beverley sister Joy, whom he met on April 13. After 'inviting her to see my trophies', he wedded her a few weeks later on July 27! But, for William Ambrose Wright, who had spent nearly 20 years in digs with Mr and Mrs Arthur Colley, the happiest day of his life was still a few months away. That was April 5 — the day he was named for his 100th England cap (the 1-0 win over Scotland at Wembley) and on which Joy presented him with their first daughter.

Despite being run ragged by Jimmy Greaves in a 6-2 defeat at Chelsea early in 1958-59, Wright was still so much at the top of his profession that it was incredible, in hindsight, that retirement was only a few months away. He missed only three League games as Wolves retained the title in style and his ever-present record with England meant he had missed only three matches for his country in the 13 years since he had made his full debut.

It was a staggering record of consistency and excellence, England winning 60, drawing 23 and losing 21 of the games he played for them. The odd one out was the 1953 meeting with Argentina in Buenos Aires, where rain stopped play after 23 minutes!

Stan Cullis subsequently described him as the man who had done more than any other to lift the social standing of the professional footballer and, on the 1959 England tour of South America, he was granted the Freedom of every Brazilian ground and presented with a two-foot high figure by the country's Press. On the same tour, he heard of his award of the CBE and successfully begged his team-mates to keep it secret until it was formally announced in the honours list. Back home at about the same time, many of the 700 tickets for a banquet in Wright's honour had to be balloted, such was the demand.

When the curtain finally came down, it was against a backcloth of great sadness and surprise. Wright had inspired Wolves to their second successive title triumph in 1958-59 and then played in all four games of the disappointing England tour of Brazil, Peru, Mexico and North America.

After his abbreviated summer's break, he returned for close-season training and went through the customary slog for fitness on the hills of Cannock Chase. But the sight of the club's youngsters speeding past him in training sowed the seeds of doubt in his mind. He had decided as a youngster that he never wanted his career to die a lingering death. He wanted a dignified exit. Was this the time to go?

'Walter Winterbottom, the England manager, had asked me on tour whether I intended retiring and I said no,' Wright added. 'But, after I returned to this country, Joy and I were invited to the Stanstead home of the Chancellor of the Exchequer, Lord Butler, on the day I received my CBE. He gave me what I later considered to be a very good piece of advice.

'He asked me whether I had ever thought of retiring and I replied by saying football had been so good to me that I wanted to stay in it. But he pointed out that he had previously been Chancellor of a Conservative Government who had a tremendous three years. He said: "If I could have retired then, I would have been the most famous Chancellor ever. But it was a four-year term and the last year was an unpopular one. I retired a very ordinary Chancellor. You should retire at the top while your mind is positive".'

A few weeks later, Wright had a chat with Stan Cullis, contacted *Express & Star* correspondent Phil Morgan and announced his retirement. 'I found I was chasing the youngsters, so training became a bind,' he added. 'All my life, I had been a hard trainer, a hard player and I gave my all because pulling on a Wolves or an England shirt meant so much. But I had had enough.'

The bombshell exploded before Wolves' traditional first team v reserves match at the start of the 1959-60 season. Cullis had the young George Showell pushing hard for Wright's first-team jersey and the 'old hand' was named for the day in the reserves. At short notice, though, Cullis switched Wright back into his first team and the great man's record of never having been relegated to the second team was still intact.

'I took a long time changing after that last game,' Wright later wrote. 'I wasn't quite able to accept the fact that I was now an ex-player. I read and re-read hundreds of goodwill messages friends from all over the world had sent me and then I realised I had the dressing-room all to myself. I pulled my coat off the corner peg on which I had hung my clothes for so long, paused to take a last look round that friendly dressing-room and then, slowly, reluctantly, I let the door swing shut. It was indeed all over.'

Apart from being the first man to win 100 full England caps, he had played in four wartime internationals, two B internationals and 21 games for the English League. With typical modesty, he reflects: 'What a career for a young lad from Ironbridge — and what a way to see the world!'

He went on to manage the England youth and under-23 teams, had a four-year stint as Arsenal manager and then worked for more than 20 years for ATV and Central TV. Now living in North London, he interrupted his retirement almost immediately a couple of years ago to become heavily involved with cable television. And it was one of the more popular off-field developments at Wolverhampton Wanderers in recent years when he was appointed to the Molineux board in May. It was a commonsense way of making sure the Billy Wright Story continued a bit longer. The memories, though, will live on forever.

FULL INTERNATIONAL CAPS (105)

(England score given first in each case)

1946: Northern Ireland (Belfast) 7-2; Eire (Dublin) 1-0; Wales (Manchester City) 3-0; Holland (Huddersfield) 8-2.

1947: Scotland (Wembley) 1-1; France (Arsenal) 3-0; Switzerland (Zürich) 0-1; Portugal (Lisbon) 10-0; Belgium (Brussels) 5-2; Wales (Cardiff) 3-0; Northern Ireland (Everton) 2-2; Sweden (Arsenal) 4-2.

1948: Scotland (Hampden) 2-0; Italy (Turin) 4-0; Denmark (Copenhagen) 0-0; Northern Ireland (Belfast) 6-2; Wales (Aston Villa) 1-0; Switzerland (Arsenal) 6-0.

1949: Scotland (Wembley) 1-3; Sweden (Stockholm) 1-3; Norway (Oslo) 4-1; France (Paris) 3-1; Eire (Everton) 0-2; Wales (Cardiff) 4-1; Northern Ireland (Manchester City) 9-2; Italy (Tottenham) 2-0.

1950: Scotland (Hampden) 1-0; Portugal (Lisbon) 5-3; Belgium (Brussels) 4-1; Chile (Rio de Janeiro) 2-0; USA (Belo Horizonte) 0-1; Spain (Rio de Janeiro) 0-1; Northern Ireland (Belfast) 4-1.

1951: Scotland (Wembley) 2-3; Argentina (Wembley) 2-1; France (Arsenal) 2-2; Wales (Cardiff) 1-1; Northern Ireland (Aston Villa) 2-0; Austria (Wembley) 2-2.

1952: Scotland (Hampden) 2-1; Italy (Florence) 1-1; Austria (Vienna) 3-2; Switzerland (Zürich) 3-0; Northern Ireland (Belfast) 2-2; Wales (Wembley) 5-2; Belgium (Wembley) 5-0.

1953: Scotland (Wembley) 2-2; Argentina (Buenos Aires) 0-0 (abandoned after 23 minutes, rain); Chile (Santiago) 2-1; Uruguay (Montevideo) 1-2; USA (New York) 6-3; Wales (Cardiff) 4-1; Rest of Europe (Wembley) 4-4; Northern Ireland (Everton) 3-1; Hungary (Wembley) 3-6.

1954: Scotland (Hampden) 4-2; Yugoslavia (Belgrade) 0-1; Hungary (Budapest) 1-7; Belgium (Basle) 4-4; Switzerland (Berne) 2-0; Uruguay (Basle) 2-4; Northern Ireland (Belfast) 2-0; Wales (Wembley) 3-2; West Germany (Wembley) 3-1.

1955: Scotland (Wembley) 7-2; France (Paris) 0-1; Spain (Madrid) 1-1; Portugal (Oporto) 1-3; Denmark (Copenhagen) 5-1; Wales (Cardiff) 1-2; Northern Ireland (Wembley) 3-0; Spain (Wembley) 4-1.

1956: Scotland (Hampden) 1-1; Brazil (Wembley) 4-2; Sweden (Stockholm) 0-0; Finland (Helsinki) 5-1; West Germany (Berlin) 3-1; Northern Ireland (Belfast) 1-1; Wales (Wembley) 3-1; Yugoslavia (Wembley) 3-0; Denmark (Wolverhampton) 5-2.

1957: Scotland (Wembley) 2-1; Eire (Wembley) 5-1; Denmark (Copenhagen) 4-1; Eire (Dublin) 1-1; Wales (Cardiff) 4-0; Northern Ireland (Wembley) 2-3; France (Wembley) 4-0.

1958: Scotland (Hampden) 4-0; Portugal (Wembley) 2-1; Yugoslavia (Belgrade) 0-5; USSR (Moscow) 1-1; USSR (Gothenburg) 2-2; Brazil (Gothenburg) 0-0; Austria (Boras) 2-2; USSR (Gothenburg) 0-1; Northern Ireland (Belfast) 3-3; USSR (Wembley) 5-0; Wales (Aston Villa) 2-2.

1959: Scotland (Wembley) 1-0; Italy (Wembley) 2-2; Brazil (Rio de Janeiro) 0-2; Peru (Lima) 1-4; Mexico (Mexico City) 1-2; USA (Los Angeles) 8-1.

Wright's 105 caps were won against the following countries: Northern Ireland 13; Scotland 13; Wales 12; France 5; Belgium 4; Denmark 4; Eire 4; Portugal 4; USSR 4; Switzerland 4; Italy 4; Spain 3; Austria 3; Sweden 3; Yugoslavia 3; Brazil 3; USA 3; Argentina 2; Chile 2; Hungary 2; West Germany 2; Uruguay 2; Finland 1; Holland 1; Norway 1; Rest of Europe 1; Peru 1; Mexico 1.

WOLVES APPEARANCES

League: 490. F.A. Cup: 48. European: 2. Charity Shield: 1. Total: 541. Goals: 16.

CHAPTER 4

Jimmy Mullen

IT'S CUSTOMARY FOR NICE THINGS TO BE SAID about the deceased but, in referring to the late Jimmy Mullen, it's difficult to find anyone with a bad word. As well as being another player with an undoubted right to a place among the Woverhampton Wanderers greats, he was a star recognised as one of the game's true gentlemen. A glorious example to any youngster hoping to follow in his hugely successful footsteps.

Mullen, a Geordie exiled by football to Wolverhampton in 1937, remained a Wolves man through and through until the end. Even in the week of his death in October, 1987, he had been at Molineux for the club's Littlewoods Cup match against Manchester City. He would still have been going today had his life not ended tragically and suddenly at the age of 64. But his spirit and the supporters' adoration of him are still very much there.

Mullen hated turning down a request to help promote the club he graced as a player for nearly a quarter of a century. Whether it meant attending a function, knocking over a pile of pennies in a pub or lending his 'pull' to the activities of the Molineux commercial department, he simply didn't like saying no. And, by those he came into contact with, he will be remembered as much for the man he was as for the player he was.

His name is still attached to a boys' football competition in the town and it's a sign of his popularity that his contemporaries were so moved by his passing-away that they set up a former players' association a few weeks later. The surviving stars of the thirties, forties and fifties, who turned out en masse to pay their last respects, didn't want their reunions to be confined to funerals as time wore on, so they arranged the first of an altogether happier series of get-togethers, which, sadly, nobody would have enjoyed more than Mullen himself.

In football terms, his greatness is unquestioned. He stands sixth behind Derek Parkin, Billy Wright, Ron Flowers, Kenny Hibbitt and Peter Broadbent with his 445 League outings for the club. His haul of 486 appearances in all competitions has been bettered by only seven others. Goals were in rich supply, too, with 112 coming his way in League and cup, while, in a highly competitive era, he picked up 12 full England caps in addition to playing three wartime internationals, making three appearances for the England B side, turning out once for the Football League and having one outing in an unofficial England World Cup XI.

As well as picking up three Football League winners' medals and an F.A. Cup winners' medal, he also has a special place in the history books as the first player to go on as substitute for England. But the statistics can only tell part of the story of the brilliant left-winger who plied his trade around England, Europe and the rest of the world from 1939 to 1959.

James Mullen was born in Newcastle-upon-Tyne on January 6, 1923, spending his youthful days either playing for Newcastle Boys and Northumberland Boys or making the short journey to watch the mighty Newcastle United at St. James's Park. It says a lot for Wolves that they were able to prise him away from the North-East at the age of 14, for the obvious move was to his hometown club. But news of the thriving youth policy run by manager Major Frank Buckley at Molineux had spread far and wide and Master Mullen was advised by one of his teachers that Wolves were the right club.

Chasing a lost cause . . . Jimmy Mullen for once kept under control as defender Stan Rickaby shields the ball from him in a Wolves v West Bromwich Albion derby at Molineux.

The new Buckley Babe, who moved South in 1937 and played for England schoolboys at about the same time, received expert grooming — and not just on the pitch. The Major insisted that his young boys should regularly show him their savings account books to prove they weren't squandering their hard-earned money! The respect they had for him also ensured they were never seen out after 10 p.m.

Their youthful ambitions were nearly destroyed before they had time to blossom, however. When Wolves realised they couldn't afford to carry on playing during the war, Buckley informed all his groundstaff boys that they would have to go. But he thought again and subsequently sent them a telegram saying: 'Return to Wolverhampton at once!'

Among Mullen's early groundstaff colleagues was a blond-haired boy who went on to travel the world with him, Billy Wright. Their careers at the time followed a remarkably similar pattern, both breaking into Wolves' first team around the war years and graduating to the England senior side in 1946-47. In addition, they briefly worked together at the Goodyear tyre company alongside their Molineux duties and both guested impressively for Leicester City during the war. But the great friendship did have one turbulent moment.

'As kids, we once came to blows at Molineux,' Wright reveals. 'Jimmy was in digs in the same street as me and an argument broke out one morning after he had shouted through the letter-box to make sure I was up. In the row that developed when we reached the ground, I broke Jimmy's nose but it wasn't all one-sided. He threw me from one side of the drying-room to the other and left me with the top of my head cracked open. But, with our wounds healed, we shook hands and always remained tremendous friends afterwards!'

Mullen's first-team debut for Wolves came as a 16-year-old in a 4-1 win at home to Leeds United on February 18, 1939, and he partly justified the faith shown in him by setting up a headed goal for Dennis Westcott after only five minutes. 'My outstanding memory of the game, though,' he said some years later, 'was the sporting attitude of the Leeds full-back, Ken Gadsby. He was a hefty fellow and I had felt some trepidation at the thought of our encounter. But, as we went out on to the field, he told me to play my normal game without fear. He assured me he wasn't out to hurt me. Throughout the match, he played me perfectly fairly and I've always felt grateful to him for not trying to destroy my confidence.'

Manager Buckley caused a sensation and made history when he fielded two 16-year-old wingers in Mullen and Alan Steen against visiting Manchester United a month later and Mullen became the youngest player ever to represent the club in an F.A. Cup semi-final when he faced Grimsby Town at Old Trafford. Initially used on the right, he had switched to his favoured left by the end of the season as Wolves narrowly lost out to Everton in the race for the title but the teenagers were absent as a side built around the tried-and-trusted Tom Galley, Stan Cullis, Joe Gardiner, Dicky Dorsett and the 43-goal

Off we go . . . Wolves' players receive a rousing send-off from fans at Molineux as they board the coach for their 1949 F.A. Cup final date with Leicester City. Players pictured are (from left) Jimmy Mullen, Sammy Smyth, Billy Crook, Johnny Hancocks, Laurie Kelly, Dennis Wilshaw, Billy Wright, Bert Williams, Roy Pritchard, Terry Springthorpe, Bill Shorthouse, Jimmy Dunn.

Westcott surprisingly crashed 4-1 against Portsmouth in the Cup final.

As war broke out, Wolves played less and less football and Mullen, who signed professional forms in 1940, went to Leicester and then Darlington to keep in trim. But he was called into the Army in 1942, first to Farnborough, then Catterick and finally Barnard Castle, Durham. There, he met up with a fellow physical training instructor Jimmy Gordon, his hero from his days on the Newcastle terraces, and went on to entertain the troops on football tours of Southern Italy and Northern Scotland.

He may have been away from the front line but he wasn't immune from danger. He suffered the most serious injury of his life when he broke his ankle playing basketball in the early 1940s and also emerged white-faced and white-knuckled from a

Dakota plane which lost an engine when bringing him and several others back from a morale-raising visit to the troops in Belgium!

All told, Mullen played 13 games for the Army, one for the F.A. Services XI, one for Combined Services (again in company with Wright) and eight for Northern Command. And he was straight back into his stride for Wolves when the cessation of hostilities allowed the resumption of the Football League. In 1946-47, he sat out only four League games in another title near-miss, his 11 goals also prompting the England selectors to invite him to further his international career.

He had already played wartime games for England against Wales (twice) and Belgium but the big senior call came for the Wembley confrontation with auld enemy Scotland on April 12, 1947. A Raich Carter goal earned England a 1-1 draw but, after being selected to face France three weeks later and then being withdrawn so he could turn out for Wolves at Portsmouth, he disappeared somewhat from the international picture. Fixtures between countries were a rarer commodity in those days and Mullen, after losing his place to Blackburn Rovers' Bobby Langton, had to wait patiently for more than two years for his second chance.

In the meantime, Mullen had to be content with performing his magic for Wolves, he and right-sided Johnny Hancocks staking a strong claim to being the finest pair of wingers in British club football. As well as both being superb crossers and strikers of the ball, they had an almost telepathic understanding which enabled them to pick each other out with raking passes from one flank to the other.

Cullis moved in as manager after Ted Vizard had led the club to final placings of third and fifth in the first two post-war seasons — and wingers were very much part of his plans. He disliked seeing either in their own half, preferring to see them operating in the areas of the field where they would inflict most damage on opponents. And inflict damage they most certainly

Proud moment . . . Mullen meets the Duke of Edinburgh at Wembley in 1949. Next in the queue are Jimmy Dunn and Jesse Pye.

did, Mullen having that rare ability to produce dangerous centres on the run and in tight areas where every avenue seemed closed.

Westcott and Jesse Pye were around to make use of the first-class service, as were Roy Swinbourne, Dennis Wilshaw and Jimmy Murray in subsequent years. But Mullen and Hancocks were also renowned marksmen themselves, scoring ten and 16 respectively in 1947-48. The mayhem continued the following season, at the end of which both players received F.A. Cup winners' medals — and further international recognition.

Mullen was among the scorers as Chesterfield capitulated 6-0 at Molineux in round three and, after Sheffield United had gone the same way, he 'presented' Liverpool's former Wolves keeper Cyril Sidlow with a welcome-home gift in the fifth round. Sidlow, who still trained at Molineux, thought he had Mullen pretty well sized up, realising he had one of the hardest left-foot shots in football and matching fire with fire by producing some fine saves from him. Then, with the tie in the balance, Mullen bore down on him again, this time transferring the ball unexpectedly to his right foot and smashing it gloriously past the stranded keeper.

Wolves were through 3-1 and, after another Mullen special had seen off Albion in a tight quarter-final at Molineux, Cullis' men came through an epic semi-final against Manchester United. Their progress to the twin towers was no surprise, though, to one young waitress at a Stafford hotel. She had served the Manchester United players 12 months earlier on their way to winning the Cup, so, when Wolves started turning up for lunch there after their customary round of golf at Brocton Hall and their swim at the nearby brine baths, she tipped them for Wembley glory, too!

In case his team-mates needed any extra motivation on arrival at the Empire Stadium, skipper Wright opened the dressing-room window shortly before kick-off and allowed the strains of 'Abide With Me' to flood in. And, sure enough, Wolves emerged victorious, 3-1 at the expense of the Leicester side he and Mullen had guested for a few years earlier, though Ken Chisholm was the only survivor of the team they knew.

A Cup winners' medal was the ideal present to take into the close season but, for Mullen, it was far from an inactive summer. He was duly named for the England tour of Sweden, Norway and France, playing in two of the games and scoring in one. His absence was for the opening match in Stockholm, where England's 3-1 defeat prompted changes — and the end of Mullen's 25-month international exile. He returned in Oslo five days later, hit one of the goals in a 4-1 victory that marked the great Frank Swift's last cap and kept his place as the French were tamed 3-1 in Paris.

The 1950 World Cup finals in Brazil were on the horizon when the following League season dawned and it was the ambition of dozens of talented young English players to be there. Mullen certainly fitted into that category but his dream

Eyes fixed on the ball, body in full flight and perfectly balanced . . . another menacing cross about to be delivered.

was in danger of fading when he was overlooked for the next six full internationals. There was no shortage of action at Wolves, though, his career haul of appearances being increased by 47 games as he helped the club to runners-up place in the

First Division and to the fifth round in their defence of the Cup.

The England selectors clearly had him down as a borderline case for he was only named as reserve for the May 18 match against Belgium at the Heysel Stadium. Then, after becoming England's first-ever substitute by going on after nine minutes for the injured Jackie Milburn in Brussels — and scoring — he was only on B international duty in Luxemburg a few days later. But he had done enough. Shortly after the squad arrived back in England, the World Cup party were announced — and Mullen was included.

Team-mates Wright and Bert Williams were also in the squad asked to attend four days' training at Dulwich Hamlet before departure while a rather unusual item went into the team luggage before lift-off, the players being fitted with soft-leather, lightweight 'Rio Boots' to help them cope with the expected hard pitches. On arrival, though, the South American turf was found to have some give, so the innovative footwear was given the order of the boot!

The Wolves trio were selected for the opening game against Chile in Rio de Janeiro, where, despite a 2-0 win amid the thunderflashes and the firecrackers, England were unimpressive. Mullen had the consolation of setting up Stan Mortensen's 37th-minute headed goal with a fine run and, with Wilf Mannion adding No. 2, the side were still being hailed as the Kings of Football — and as certainties to brush aside the challenge of the USA in the next game. The Americans were rated no better than a good English Third Division side and the hundreds of locally-based British workers had lodged big-money bets on the outcome when they turned up in anticipation of a landslide victory.

But, in one of the most famous upsets in post-war soccer, England had virtually all the play and lost 1-0. The game was played in the city of Belo Horizonte, which, when translated, means Beautiful Horizon. But the outlook was suddenly decidedly gloomy as the players made their way the 280 miles back to their Copacabana Beach headquarters in Rio.

As he would like to be remembered . . . the late, great Jimmy Mullen striding past a stranded opponent.

It was so stiflingly hot that training could only take place before noon and after 3.30 p.m. and certain members of the Press had given the players such a hot reception after the defeat at the hands of the weakest team in the tournament that one player said: 'I wish they would give me a badge explaining I was only a non-playing reserve!'

Mullen was left out of the decisive game against Spain in Rio, where England's unhappy trip was rounded off by a 1-0 defeat. The watching masses found it impossible to accept the tournament was losing its star attraction so early, many spectators standing up and waving their handkerchiefs amid a sad rendition of Adios in the dying minutes of the game. Unbelievably, England were on their way home and Mullen was to face a long absence from the international limelight.

He returned home to open a sports shop in Wolverhampton town centre several weeks later and could have modelled much of the gear he and Joan — his wife of four years — were selling. As well as possessing one of the hardest shots in football, he had astonishing speed and, like keeper Williams, could cover 100 yards in ten seconds. His 5ft 10in, 11st 4lb physique was almost perfect for an athlete and, despite temporary England rejection, he was clearly a long way from being finished.

He took his League and cup goal tally past 50 during a lean 1950-51 season that ended with a final placing of 14th and, in an even more mediocre campaign for the club 12 months later, he returned with Wolves to St. James's Park, Newcastle, to make his 200th Football League appearance. Still, he was virtually an ever-present, his 250th League game coming at home to Preston North End a season later as Wolves again began to emerge as a major force.

He was still out in the cold with England, however. He hadn't played since the humiliation against the Americans in Brazil, his exile stretching to more than three years before he was called up for his seventh cap. His comeback was against Wales at Cardiff on October 10, 1953, and so eye-catching was his contribution in making three of his side's goals in a 4-1 win that he was retained for the Wembley clash with a Rest of Europe side 11 days later.

And, this time, Mullen turned goalscorer, inspiring a recovery from 3-1 down and helping salvage a 4-4 draw by tapping into an empty net just before half-time and rifling in the rebound from Stanley Matthews' blocked shot just after the interval. England were again among the goals when the Wolves winger lined up in the game against Northern Ireland at Goodison Park and, although he missed both of the crushing defeats at the hands of Hungary, he played and scored in the 4-2 away win against Scotland in between and also turned out in the defeat in Yugoslavia.

His tally of full caps stood at 11 and Wolves' return to prominence ensured he remained in the spotlight. He played another 38 League games, scoring seven goals, as Wolves became champions for the first time in 1953-54 with a side largely bred, if not born, in the West Midlands. Mullen,

All dressed up and rarin' to go . . . Wolves line up before turning on the style to beat Derby County 2-0 at the Baseball Ground in August, 1950. Back row from left: Billy Crook, Roy Pritchard, Ray Chatham, Bert Williams, Roy Swinbourne, Angus McLean. Front: Jimmy Dunn, Johnny Walker, Billy Wright, Jesse Pye, Jimmy Mullen.

however, was intensely proud of his Tyneside roots, not only retaining his distinct Geordie accent but also ribbing his team-mates with gentle reminders that all the top clubs seemed to have a North-Easterner or two in their midst!

Seven of Wolves' 1953-54 title-winning team went on to make more than 300 League appearances for the club and eight members of the Molineux staff figured in all three championship triumphs in the 1950s. It was a remarkable demonstration of their loyalty in Wolverhampton Wanderers with Mullen, as much as anyone, thanking his lucky stars for having opted to join them.

'Jimmy was a real gentleman on and off the field and was always grateful to football for giving him a good living,' Cullis says. 'He gave everything for the club and was always willing to sacrifice his private time for charity work. If I was asked to provide a player for a hospital visit or to open a garden fete,

Jimmy was always among the first to volunteer. I needed the players to be good at things other than football, like acting as ambassadors for the town and being part of the community. And he was one of the best.'

As the doting father of a son and daughter, he was also immensely popular with the young players at the club, always full of good advice and often chosen to give nervous newcomers a tour of the ground on their first day. He typified just the sort of atmosphere Cullis was trying to create at Molineux because junior players would look up to him and his contemporaries with the realisation: 'He's a star because he has the right attitude. He isn't cocky with his success, so what have I got to be cocky about'?'

A Wolves side without Gentleman Jim was unthinkable but there was one final senior England outing before, at the age of 31, he resigned himself to a diet of club football only. That international farewell came, complete with his sixth goal for his country, in England's 2-0 World Cup finals victory over Switzerland in Berne on June 29, 1954. Wolves team-mate Dennis Wilshaw scored in the same match but England went out in the quarter-finals and the presence of rivals like Matthews, Tom Finney and Frank Blunstone forced Mullen on to the international sidelines for good.

Not that his travelling days were over. As well as making a further 120-plus League and cup appearances for Wolves, he figured strongly in their floodlit triumphs and flew with them to such varied parts of the world as South Africa twice, Russia and virtually every country in Western Europe.

After helping them to second, third and sixth places in 1954-55, 1955-56 and 1956-57 respectively, there were also two more League championship medals to be picked up in the following two years. He totalled 54 First Division games over the two triumphant campaigns, also playing twice in the club's brief entry into the European Cup in 1958-59.

He didn't figure in the more successful run to the semi-final in the same competition 12 months later but still played in some epic European games. It didn't seem to matter that the matches were only friendlies for, in an age when televisions were non-existent in most households, fans poured into grounds in their tens of thousands to savour the only real chance they had to see their heroes.

Wolves were still a huge pull on their travels as well, spreading their wings far and wide in the 1950s to take on the likes of First Vienna, Valencia, Anderlecht, Real Madrid, Grasshoppers Zürich and Stuttgart. In a magnificent 2-2 draw against European champions Madrid in December, 1957, Mullen hit the post five minutes from time — but Wolves' players still thought they had something to celebrate.

Cullis was a stickler for punctuality and discipline but his charges took it upon themselves to go out and paint the city a pale shade of red after the post-match banquet had ended soon after midnight. With the message going round the room that the coach was about to leave for the hotel, the players had devised an alternative plan. They rose to a man, as if to file out to the bus, but made instead for a local nightclub where they remained until the not-so-early hours. They braced themselves next morning for a blast from their manager but Cullis — out of character — merely replied: 'Why didn't you tell me where you were going? I would have gone as well!'

As the end of his career approached, Mullen was prevented by a cartilage injury from going on a club tour to Germany and Switzerland and was also coming under pressure of a different kind — from players like Des Horne, Norman Deeley and Micky Lill. He made 18 appearances in 1958-59 and few would have believed when he walked off at the end of the home draw with Tottenham on March 2, 1959, that they had just seen him for the last time in a senior game.

Although he remained at the club in the following season, he wasn't picked again, leaving him to retire with an agonising 98 League goals to his name. Mullen, whose brother Andrew had briefly been on Villa's books before moving to Workington and Scunthorpe United, duly retired in that season, so breaking Wolves' last playing link with the pre-wa days.

He left with the same grace that he had shown throughou his career, telling guests at the testimonial match he shared witl Wright in 1962: 'If I had a son good enough to play football there's no club I would want him to play for other thar Wolverhampton Wanderers.' He also received a special trophy from the Football League to mark more than 20 years' service to one club and, as a man who didn't drink and didn't swear, he could have been held up as an example to millions of young hopefuls.

Mullen, who had taken an F.A. course, later passed on some of his knowledge by coaching Midlands youngsters. But he spent most of his time at his thriving sports shop, where sales of plimsolls soared one day during the early years of football hooliganism. A group of visiting fans were refused admission to Molineux because they were wearing 'bovver' boots, so they made a bee-line for his shop to buy something more acceptable!

A decade and a half on, he and his wife sold their shop and Gentleman Jim had just a year of retirement before, in 1987, came the news that saddened and shocked the area's footballing public. To many, he was THE hero among a team of heroes, his appeal best summed up in this poignant poem from supporter John McLeod:

Goodbye Jimmy Mullen, star of my youth,
Always the gentleman, never uncouth,
What pleasure you gave us in days gone by,
It only seems yesterday, how the years fly.

I remember with pride, the memories flood back,
When Wolves were the kings in old gold and black,
With players like Hancocks, Williams and Wright,
Rival fans stood together and applauded the sight.

To live in the past is not always good,
Oh, bring back the good times, if only we could,
But it's the end of an era to tell you the truth,
So, goodbye, Jimmy Mullen, star of my youth.

FULL INTERNATIONAL CAPS (12)

(England score given first in each case)

1947: Scotland (Wembley) 1-1.

1949: Norway (Oslo) 4-1; France (Paris) 3-1.

1950: Belgium (Brussels) 4-1; Chile (Rio de Janeiro) 2-0; USA (Belo Horizonte) 0-1.

1953: Wales (Cardiff) 4-1; Rest of Europe (Wembley) 4-4; Northern Ireland (Everton) 3-1.

1954: Scotland (Hampden) 4-2; Yugoslavia (Belgrade) 0-1; Switzerland (Berne) 2-0.

WOLVES APPEARANCES

League: 445. F.A. Cup: 38. European: 2. Charity Shield: 1. Total: 486. Goals: 112.

CHAPTER 5

Johnny Hancocks

THIRTY-THREE YEARS INTO HIS RETIREMENT from League football, Johnny Hancock is happy to explode one of Molineux's great myths. He never wore size two boots!

The little man with the great cannonball of a shot took a size six boot — and wore an extra wide one at that. Where the story about tiny feet came from, he isn't quite sure. But he can confirm it isn't true.

'Virtually every newspaper story I've ever had written about me seems to have said I took size two boots,' he said. 'We've had a laugh about it over the years, especially when our daughter Helen read an article about me earlier this year and asked if my feet had grown since my playing days. I told her they hadn't. In fact, the smallest I ever wore was a six.'

It wasn't only the size of Hancocks' feet, however, which caused confusion. Opponents were often in a daze against his trickery, pace and ferocious shooting — attributes which made him a fearsome winger in post-war soccer and very much part of the emergence of Wolverhampton Wanderers as one of the best and most famous teams in the world.

All told, he scored 168 goals in 378 Wolves appearances between 1946 and 1956 and won three England caps along the way. But considerably more international recognition would have been heaped upon him had he not had the misfortune to

Hard and true . . . a Hancocks penalty.

be weaving his magic in the same era as Tom Finney and the legendary Sir Stanley Matthews.

Hancocks, who also made two appearances in the Football League side, cost a meagre £4,000 when he moved to Molineux from neighbouring Walsall on May 11, 1946. Like goalkeeper Bert Williams, who made the same short journey just after the end of the war, he was to repay Wolves' faith many times over.

Johnny had played as a centre-half and then an inside-left as a lad and progressed via the Wrekin schools team to a place in the Oakengates side in the Birmingham League. From there, he joined Walsall in October, 1938, figured in their journey to the F.A. Cup fifth round that season and followed wartime games as a guest for Wrexham and Shrewsbury Town by playing in the Saddlers' Third Division South Cup final against Bournemouth at Chelsea shortly afterwards.

That was his last game for Walsall and he signed for Wolves the day before Jesse Pye did likewise — both of them in time to go on the club's summer trip to Sweden in 1946. Some weeks later, he played his first League game in the famous old gold in the sort of match that was to become the club's hallmark in their glory years — a 6-1 slaughter of Arsenal in front of 50,845 enthralled spectators on August 31. He didn't score that day, leaving the goals to be shared among Pye (3),

Dennis Westcott (2) and Jimmy Mullen. But it wasn't too long before his scoring prowess became evident.

He broke his duck in another 6-1 home romp, this time against hapless Huddersfield Town, and followed up with the only goal of the game when Leeds United visited Molineux a week later. Under the managership of the man who signed him, Ted Vizard, he finished that 1946/47 season with ten goals in 40 League games, including a purple patch of five in six in the spring.

Hancocks, who also found the target in one of the club's three F.A. Cup games that winter, could easily have ended his first season at Molineux with a championship medal. But Britain suffered a particularly harsh winter and Wolves went a frustrating 35 days without playing a League game. When the temperature finally rose, the side's hopes plummeted with defeats at Sheffield United, Manchester United and Derby County in the space of barely a fortnight putting the brakes on their title drive.

But they bounced back by crushing Derby 7-2, Bolton Wanderers 3-0 and Chelsea 6-4 — a trio of matches which yielded four goals for the flying winger. A 1-0 win at Huddersfield, secured when Hancocks converted the rebound from his own saved penalty, left Wolves top after the penultimate game and meant English football's most sought-after prize was at their fingertips when arch rivals Liverpool came to town on Saturday, May 31 — a date when footballers were traditionally putting their feet up for a few weeks' break. Victory would have left Wolves home and dry as champions while a draw might have done the trick if Stoke were to slip up against Sheffield United.

As on the opening day of the season exactly nine months earlier, more than 50,000 packed into Molineux, with an estimated 40,000 queuing in the baking sunshine outside the ground at 12.30 p.m.! The temperature was recorded at 1 p.m. as a staggering 96 degrees (79 in the shade) and the awe-inspiring sense of drama intensified further when an emotional

The pleasure's all mine . . . Hancocks meeting the Duke of Gloucester before the 1949 F.A. Cup final against Leicester City. Wolves players in the foreground are Jesse Pye and Jimmy Dunn.

loudspeaker announcement 15 minutes before kick-off relayed the news that this was to be Stan Cullis's last match as a player.

Unhappily, it all went wrong for Wolves after 3 p.m. as they fell 2-0 behind in the first half and were repeatedly frustrated by their former keeper Cyril Sidlow, now in the Liverpool goal. Jimmy Dunn set up a grandstand finish with a goal midway through the second period, but Wolves were unable to break through a second time and their fans streamed home disappointed. Liverpool had gone top — a position they held despite Stoke's game in hand — and Wolves were even pipped to runners-up spot on goal average by Manchester United.

'That game was one of the saddest I ever played in for Wolves,' Hancocks said. 'Everything was set up for Stan Cullis to pick up the League championship trophy in his last game, but it wasn't to be. We had gone to Blackpool to prepare for the game and went out to Sutton Coldfield for our pre-match meal, so we could escape the supporters! I can remember the great disappointment afterwards. It could have been one long celebration among the players and crowd but, as it turned out, we couldn't get home quickly enough.'

Wolves' team that day was Williams, McLean, Crook, Alderton, Cullis, Wright, Hancocks, Dunn, Pye, Forbes, Mullen, the notable exception being centre-forward Dennis Westcott, whose 38 League goals that season — eight ahead of his nearest First Division rival — were a club record, threatened more than 40 years later by Steve Bull's 37 in 1988-89. It wasn't much consolation, either, that Wolves were the season's top scorers in the top flight with 98.

Hancocks ended his first season at the club with 11 goals and continued to click as a taker, as well as a maker, in another fruitless title chase in 1947-48. His tally of 16 left him tied at the top of the club's scoring charts with Pye and included a goal in each of Wolves' first five games of the season. That was perhaps no great feat, though, considering the side's opening results were 3-4, 8-1, 5-1, 4-0 and 2-2!

In a season in which he made 40 League and Cup appearances, inconsistent Wolves saved their best until last, reeling off four successive wins in April in a futile pursuit of Arsenal. By coincidence, they again lost 2-1 to Liverpool in their last match — this time a less decisive fixture at Anfield — but had the consolation of finishing in the top five for the fifth successive season.

Hancocks had emerged as a feared penalty-taker but his rare miss from the spot in the fourth-round tie at home to Everton contributed to the end of Wolves' Cup hopes for another season. 'It's one of only a couple of penalties I can remember missing,' he recalls. 'I didn't worry too much about placing my kicks. I went for power and then hoped the goalkeeper chose not to get his body behind them!

'Most of the goals I scored were shots. There weren't many headers because of my size. And a lot of my goals were

A two-man lift . . . Hancocks and Wright with the League championship trophy they helped win in 1953-54.

thanks to Jimmy Mullen. I lost count of the times he picked me out with his crosses.'

The summer of 1948 was a watershed in the club's post-war history. Vizard resigned as manager and, after a season serving his apprenticeship as assistant, Cullis stepped into the job he was to occupy for 16 years — most of them with great success. And his first season ended in glory with what

Hancocks described as one of his most memorable matches for the club.

Wolves again performed with great credit to finish sixth in the First Division but it was in the F.A. Cup that they thrilled the nation with a crusade that was to end in victory against Leicester City at Wembley on April 30, 1949. Ten years earlier, Wolves — then captained by Cullis — had lost against all the odds to Portsmouth in the final but there were no mistakes second time round as the club captured their first major honour for more than 40 years.

By the time Wolves went up Wembley Way, Hancocks was en route for a 12-goal League haul that was to leave him behind Pye (17) and Sammy Smyth (16) as their third leading scorer. And, like the animals on Noah's Ark, he was inclined to do things two by two, scoring braces against Bolton. Sunderland, Manchester United and Huddersfield, even before autumn had taken a proper grip. Then he collected a double in the early days of the Cup campaign, joining Jimmy Dunn on the scoresheet in a 3-0 fourth-round win at Sheffield United after Chesterfield had been hit for six in the third round.

Hancocks was to score only once more for Wolves that season — in a 2-1 Molineux success over Preston North End — but he was a vital contributor to their journey to Wembley, playing in every game as Liverpool, West Bromwich Albion and semi-final opponents Manchester United joined their list of casualties. United proved particularly awkward customers in an epic battle but finally succumbed when Smyth crashed home the only goal of the Goodison Park replay after a 1-1 draw at Hillsborough in the original game.

So Wolves were back at the twin towers and Billy Wright duly picked up the Cup from the young Princess Elizabeth after a marvellous 3-1 win. To use a cricket term, Hancocks didn't trouble the scorers but had the satisfaction of teeing up a header for the first of Pye's two goals, Smyth netting the other. And when the cavalcade returned to Wolverhampton the following day, he won the hearts of the tens of thousands on

Spot-on again . . . powering a penalty through the gloom.

the streets below when he had to be lifted up by Cullis and Wright to be fully visible above the microphones on the town hall balcony!

'It was a great, great day, a great few weeks really,' Hancocks says. 'It was billed as the Midlands match of the decade in the papers and the fans certainly treated it as though it was. The interest was fantastic and playing in a Cup final is something I'll never forget. The homecoming was the same. The streets were a sea of black and gold — it was an occasion to bring a lump to your throat.'

Wolves, who had indulged in the traditional Wembley practice of spending a couple of nights preparing in the South-East — their choice being a hotel in Weybridge, Surrey — were now boasting a side bristling with internationals. Smyth was busily collecting Irish caps and Wright was safely installed as England captain. Mullen and keeper Bert Williams joined their club skipper for the game against France in Paris in the summer of 1949, Mullen was also a team-mate of his in the match against Norway in Oslo and Dennis Wilshaw acted as reserve for the same trip to Scandinavia. But Wolves had another full England international by this time — Johnny Hancocks.

His big call-up came for the match against Switzerland at Arsenal a few months earlier — on December 1, 1948. And, as Steve Bull was to do more than 40 years later, he marked his inclusion in the best possible way. The Swiss were mere cannon fodder, in fact, crashing to a 6-0 defeat in which he scored twice and in which Wright also featured.

Hancocks went on to pick up a further two full caps at the rate of one per season. He played in a World Cup qualifier in the 4-1 slaughter of Wales at Cardiff nearly a year later and then had to wait another 13 months for his next call-up — for a draw against Yugoslavia back at Highbury. 'I was one of the smallest players ever to play for England,' he said. 'I've heard it said that I would rather have played more for Wolves on the left than I did, so I might have won more caps. But I didn't see it that way. I didn't mind which wing I played on. And I was just happy to have played at all for my country — not too many do.'

Back at Molineux, with the F.A. Cup adorning the side-board, Wolves reeled off nine wins and two draws in their first 11 games of 1949-50, again putting themselves in sight of lifting the Football League title for the first time in their history. Hancocks scored important goals against Albion and Stoke as the drama unfolded and struck again against Manchester City and Bolton as Wolves finished the season virtually as they had started it — with four wins and a draw in their last five games. Unbelievably though, the championship had eluded them by a third of a goal, Portsmouth emerging victorious on goal average as they beat Aston Villa on the tense last Saturday of the season. The frequent updates from Fratton Park, where Pompey ran out 5-1 winners, made it another afternoon of anti-climax at Molineux, from where the *Express & Star* correspondent 'Commentator' wrote of the 6-1 slaughter of Birmingham City: 'As things turned out, Wolves needed to win

20-1.' And he added later: 'Hancocks remained the only forward not to score and we saw that most unusual spectacle — a penalty miss by him.'

Wolves, meanwhile, struggled in their defence of the F.A. Cup, being taken to second games by Plymouth Argyle and Sheffield United — replays in which Hancocks totalled three crucial goals. But he and his colleagues were sadly off target in round five, where Blackpool held on for a goalless draw at Molineux before edging home 1-0 in the replay at Bloomfield Road. So Wolves ended another largely successful season empty-handed as far as the major prizes were concerned, even having to share the Charity Shield with Portsmouth at Highbury, where Hancocks provided another example of his goalscoring flair.

'Hancky' had rattled in another 14 goals over the season and had developed a thrilling, almost telepathic, understanding with left-winger Mullen. Nobody could say Wolves' style contained any unneccessary frills but, within Cullis' policy of launching the ball forward at the earliest opportunity, the wizards of the wing had the rare ability to pick each other out with long raking passes from flank to flank.

Hancocks looked supremely fit, capable of running all day — no surprise, then, that he had spent part of the wartime as a physical training instructor corporal at 20ITC Shrewsbury, helping the side win the Harley Cup three years in succession, as well as the Shropshire Junior Cup and the Shrewsbury and District League and Cup. It was in these surroundings, where he scored a regimental record of 78 goals in 1942, that he played for the first time in the same side as Wright. The liaison was to continue with Wolves for some time yet.

Hancocks chose Wolves' worst League season since 1935-36 to record his highest goal tally yet, scoring 19 times in the League in 1950-51 — one fewer than Roy Swinbourne. He also blasted his first Wolves hat-trick in a 3-1 victory over visiting Albion as 15 of his goals came by the turn of the year.

The Oakengates-born winger would definitely have played

more often for his country had he not 'graduated' at the same time as such stars as Matthews, Finney and Bobby Langton. And he may have been more strongly considered had it not been for his dislike of flying — an aversion which led to him withdrawing from one Football Association continental tour and from Wolves trips to Ireland and Brussels. 'I would rather have gone by boat really,' Johnny adds. 'I got out of one or two trips, although I would fly if I had to and went with Wolves on visits to Sweden and America.'

A team-mate revealed, however: 'Johnny wasn't too happy about travelling by any means. We were all ill on the trip to Sweden because the crossing was so rough and, even on the coach to away games, he would sit on the first double seat behind the driver and look a lot happier once we had arrived!'

Sadly, 1950-51 proved the end of his international career, although he was to play League football for another five years. He nurtured hopes of another Cup final appearance at Wembley until Newcastle United squeezed there in Wolves' place in a 1950-1 semi-final replay at Huddersfield but, after a couple of quiet seasons, his and Wolves' fortunes soared again in 1953-54.

Success had not been far away in 1952-53 as Wolves finished third in the table — but they went two better 12 months later as they lifted the title for the first time. The fact that local rivals Albion were their closest challengers provided the season with an extra touch of spice, the men from the Hawthorns finally having to settle for runners-up and the not inconsiderable consolation of beating Preston in the F.A. Cup final.

Hancocks was an ever-present, wearing his No. 7 shirt in every game apart from the crucial April 3 win at Albion, where he switched to No. 11! And he rattled in a personal best 24 goals, including a hat-trick in a memorable 8-1 Molineux mauling of Chelsea — still the Londoners' all-time record defeat — and a rare header as Wolves at last turned Highbury into a happy hunting ground. Hancocks scored 19 of his goals

Lining up before a game at Sheffield . . . From left: Angus McLean, Bill Shorthouse, Bert Williams, Roy Pritchard, Jesse Pye, Billy Wright, Sammy Smyth, Willie Forbes, Jimmy Mullen, Johnny Hancocks.

in a magnificent personal 21-match run, which also contained some outstanding team performances. Wolves went 18 League games without defeat and reeled off 14 consecutive home League victories in a run that had started at the end of the previous campaign.

There were a few flutters in the springtime but a 2-0 Roy Swinbourne-inspired win at home to Tottenham Hotspur in the last game left Wolves champions by four points. With the best goals for and goals against records (96 and 56 respectively), they were undisputed as England's best side. But were they necessarily the club's best-ever team? When asked who Wolves' best players were in his time, Johnny answers: 'All 11 of them! Bert Williams, Billy Wright, Jimmy Mullen and Bill Shorthouse spring to mind from that 1953-54 team but I also think there were some tremendous players from a few years earlier. Players like Billy Crook, Sammy Smyth, Dennis Westcott and Jimmy Dunn.'

As time moved on, 1954-55 — even by Wolves' sky-high

standards — was a memorable season. Not in terms of trophies, because the club were League runners-up, beaten Cup quarter-finalists and joint holders of the Charity Shield with Albion. No, the real memories of that season for those lucky enough to remember it are provided by the floodlit matches which extended Wolves' fame all over Europe.

Goals rained in at Molineux as if they were going out of fashion and the little fellow on the wing was at the heart of so many of their golden attacking moments. Cullis used to castigate him if he tried to play football in Wolves' half of the field — he wanted him in the opponents' half instead. But he once had good reason to regret the doubts he had over the player's penalty-taking ability.

'I bet him something like sixpence that he couldn't beat me with six penalties out of six in training,' Cullis recalls. 'He took the first two or three and I don't think I even saw them as they screamed into the net. Then, for the fourth, I moved early and had the misfortune to get my hand to it. The ball still went in and I was having treatment off the physio, George Palmer, for a fortnight!

'On another occasion, Johnny showed his accuracy by saying he could chip at will against the crossbar. He missed by inches with his first attempt but hit the bar smack on with his second. Not bad considering he was chipping from 60 yards away!'

Hancocks, now 71 and living in the same Oakengates street that he was brought up in, topped Wolves' scoring charts again in 1955-56 and had reserved a place in the Molineux hall of fame by reaching double figures in each of the ten seasons since the war. He stands third behind only John Richards (194) and Billy Hartill (170) in the list of the club's all-time top scorers and is second to Hartill in League goals alone. With 378 appearances to his name, he is 15th in the roll-call of senior games for the club.

In many ways, the decision of Cullis's to release him in the summer of 1957 was a surprise. After all, he had showed his scoring touch was still there by rattling in 24 goals for the reserves in his last season at Molineux. But it was a time of transition and Harry Hooper and Norman Deeley had emerged as contenders for the little maestro's role. Hancocks moved on to Wellington Town as player-manager and had time for spells with Cambridge United, Oswestry and GKN Sankey before the curtain came down on his outstanding playing career.

From there, he worked outside the game, notably at RAF Cosford, and again showed he was a fine all-round sportsman. Having twice had trials with Worcestershire as a wicketkeeper-batsman in his earlier years, he now found the time to become a superb bowler — of the bowling green variety. His talents, clearly, were not confined to football.

FULL INTERNATIONAL CAPS (3)

(England score given first)

1948: Switzerland (Arsenal) 6-0.
1949: Wales (Cardiff) 4-1.
1950: Yugoslavia (Arsenal) 2-2.

WOLVES APPEARANCES

League: 343. F.A. Cup: 33. Charity Shield: 2. Total: 378.
Goals: 168.

CHAPTER 6

Bert Williams

WHICHEVER WAY YOU LOOK AT IT, WHATEVER your criteria, Bert Williams really is Wolves' all-time number one number one! Untouchable as the club's finest goalkeeper ever.

Noel George was a hero of his day, Malcolm Finlayson was an impressive performer towards the end of Molineux's golden years, Phil Parkes was a fine servant and Mark Kendall made history in 1987-88 as the Wolves keeper to keep the most clean sheets in a season. But Williams, 'The Cat', was the prince of goalkeepers, the man to put them all in the shade.

He won 24 England caps, picked up a League championship medal and F.A. Cup winners' medal with Wolves and is one of the best keepers ever produced by England. In an age of great sportsmanship, he was also a gentleman — and one whose business sense, diligence and popularity leave him even more successful and well-off outside the game than he ever was in it.

His phenomenal Wolves career spanned 420 games, 381 of them in the First Division, and there were no secrets to his success. He was one of the old-fashioned school, a believer in down-to-earth values like hard work, sacrifice and total dedication. He didn't drink, he didn't smoke and he didn't indulge in another social pastime that may loosely be regarded as a vice — dancing. 'I never used to go out dancing,' he says.

Flying Machine . . . all agility and poise.

'I always used to be in bed by about quarter to ten. I believed physical fitness and mental alertness to be absolutely essential and I didn't want to do anything that would threaten my sharpness.'

It was once said of Williams, now 70, that he never admitted to being beaten by a great shot or a great header. Somewhere in his mind, he was always tortured by the belief that he could — maybe should — have prevented the goal. 'I was a perfectionist,' he adds. 'I used to hate to have goals scored against me and took them as a personal affront. I wasn't a bad loser but I detested losing! That's why the mistakes seem to stand out more than anything else from my playing career.'

Williams was born on January 31, 1920, among the factories and chimney tops of Bradley, progressing from school in nearby Bilston to play for Wolverhampton works side Thompsons. He found work in a factory at Great Bridge and was, he admits, 'a cheeky kid'. But Walsall manager Andy Wilson had seen enough of his on-field self-assurance to convince him he should sign him. He did just that and, in the formative days of the then 15-year-old's Fellows Park career, Harry Wait emerged as an excellent teacher. Williams was later taken under the wing of the new manager, former Birmingham City and England keeper Harry Hibbs, and the 'pupil' was in Walsall's first team at 16.

Wait and Hibbs may have taught him some of the tricks of his new trade but they obviously didn't provide him with a bus timetable. Williams was once waiting at a bus stop on his way to a Christmas Day home match against Bristol Rovers when a bystander shouted: 'You'll have a long wait. They aren't running today!' The young protégé still made it in time for kick-off but only after walking and running the six miles from his home! Just as well he was one of the quickest players in British football — as proven by his considerable feat of once running 100 yards in ten seconds in the Staffordshire Athletics Championships.

Williams, graduating via the Saddlers reserves, had just established himself in the first team when wartime arrived. Like so many of his contemporaries, he lost a fair chunk of his career to the demands of the services, although he was still to catch the eye sufficiently to earn a couple of unofficial England caps in victory and wartime internationals against France and Wales in 1945-46. He volunteered for the RAF and saw much of the world before returning home as determined as ever to make the grade as a professional footballer.

The onset of hostilities changed the face of the British game, however, and, among the many other differences to the pre-1939 version, players were allowed to guest for other clubs. Williams chose Nottingham Forest and Chelsea and it was during his outings for the Londoners that he decided he would join them permanently. 'I had been with Johnny Hancocks at Walsall but there was a fair bit of activity in the transfer market as the war drew towards a close. People were realising that football would soon start to return to normal. I had enjoyed playing for Chelsea during the war and it was my intention to sign for them. But everything changed when I came back up to play for Walsall during one of my weekends off from the RAF.

'After the game, the directors asked me into the boardroom because a club wanted to speak to me. I thought: "Oh good, it's Chelsea!" But it wasn't. It was Wolves. I was introduced to their secretary, Jack Howley, and I told him I wasn't interested in signing for them. I hadn't even seen them play. But Jack was very nice about it and suggested I might like to go home and discuss the matter with my wife.

'They said they would wait at the ground for me to return and I set off into the evening. I didn't have a car in those days, so it meant catching one bus to Darlaston and another to Bilston, where we lived. It was the same lengthy journey going back to Fellows Park and it must have been three hours after the final whistle when I finally arrived again at the ground. Jack Howley was still there and I signed there and then for Wolves for about £3,500. It was the best thing I ever did in my football life. My wife, Evelyn, and I had decided we didn't want to lose our Black Country roots.'

Chelsea felt a little let down by his change of mind, though, their disappointment certainly not being eased as Wolves beat them 2-1, 6-4 and 1-0 in the first three post-war meetings of the clubs. Williams, signed in September, 1945, at a time when Ted Vizard held the managerial reins, played his first League game at Molineux on the same day as Hancocks —

in the 6-1 thumping of Arsenal on August 31, 1946 — and accumulated more than 40 appearances in each of his first two seasons at the club.

He played 44 more in Wolves' F.A. Cup-winning season of 1948-49, including the 3-1 Wembley victory over Leicester City, and it was inevitable that his tremendous agility, bravery and judgement would earn him further recognition for his country. Already in that season, he had made his solitary appearance for England B — in the game against Finland. And, on May 22 in Paris, he took over in the full England side from Manchester City's Frank Swift. It was a fitting switch because Wolves manager Stan Cullis, who described Williams as 'tense and highly strung before games', also rated him the second best goalkeeper he had ever seen, after Swift.

After the 3-1 win over the French, the keeper's jersey remained proudly in possession of the new boy for the 2-0 defeat by the Republic of Ireland at Everton four months later and for the flattering Jackie Milburn-inspired 4-1 win over Wales at Cardiff in mid-October. Williams was overcoming the international claims of Tottenham's Ted Ditchburn but an injury in the Welsh game, which took place on the same day as Wolves' 1-1 First Division draw with Albion at Molineux, kept him out of three club games and the international against Northern Ireland at Maine Road four weeks later.

Williams didn't have to worry, though, for he was recalled by the selectors for the game against World Cup holders Italy at Tottenham on November 30, 1949 — and responded with probably the best performance of his career. England won 2-0 but the Press and virtually the entire 71,527 crowd were united in their belief that the Italians were the better side, prevented from becoming the first overseas nation ever to beat England in this country, only by Williams' brilliance.

Headlines such as 'Bert Williams was England hero' and 'Williams saves England record' adorned two of the following day's newspapers while the much-respected Roy Peskett wrote in the *Daily Mail*: 'Williams was magical. His clutching hands

Stepping up a class . . . Williams is dwarfed by England goalkeeper rival Frank Swift as they line up before the international against France in Paris in 1949 — the Wolves keeper's senior debut in the national side. Also there from Wolves are Billy Wright, Dennis Wilshaw (back row far right) and Jimmy Mullen (front row far right).

and flying body seemed to draw the ball to his yellow jersey. Twice he dived for a ball and changed direction in mid-air as it was diverted by a desperate defender. And twice the crowd thundered their relief as his groping fingers stopped what looked like being a certain score.'

Cullis, who described Williams' performance that day as the best he had ever seen from a goalkeeper, witnessed further heroics from his last line of defence in the next week. First, he saw him stop a ferocious penalty from Arsenal right-back Wally Barnes in a 1-1 draw at Highbury — a save that led to Williams being mobbed by his team-mates and applauded off the field by the Gunners fans. Then, only two days later, he produced the perfect follow-up by saving another spot-kick, this time from a player by the name of Tabram in a 3-0 friendly win at Merthyr Tydfil.

'It was quite a happy few days,' Williams added. 'I had a lot to do in the Italy game and loved every second of it. I did fairly well and the things that were written about me afterwards were very nice. That was the origin of the "Big Cat" nickname, or "Il Gattone", as the Italian fans and journalists called me.'

Williams was to be an ever-present in the England side for the next two years, his place on the plane to Brazil for the 1950 World Cup finals already secure as he made the first of his five appearances in the Football League side. That was in 1949-50, a season in which Wolves finished second in the League and reached the fifth round in a creditable but unsuccessful defence of the F.A. Cup.

At Molineux, his consistency sorely tested the patience of his deputies, Nigel Sims and Dennis Parsons, two men who had to wait for injury or international calls to give them an opportunity in the first team. Certainly, they were unable to dislodge Bertram Frederick Williams on merit.

Although he saw plenty of foreign goalkeepers at close quarters during his trips abroad with Wolves and England, Williams disliked the flamboyance of many of his continental counterparts. He disapproved of their tendency to punch, believing the ball was there to be fisted only if he was under severe pressure and a clean catch was impossible. Even then, he insisted on punching with both hands, not just one.

'Goalkeeping is a combination of art and science,' he once wrote in his regular column in the *Daily Express*. 'But there's one essential — physical fitness. The average fan has the idea that height and weight are the first essentials of good goalkeeping. This is pure fallacy. Perfection can't be reached without absolute physical fitness.'

Hence, the 5ft 10¼in Wolves star sprinted regularly to develop strong calf muscles (to facilitate jumping or diving from a standing position), worked frequently at a punch-ball (to sharpen his eye for a moving ball) and spent hours studying the angles at which he should defend his goal. Cycling was out because it left him heavy-legged but good judgement was definitely in. 'Come out at the right moment and the fans will love you and the Press will praise you,' he added. 'Come out at the wrong moment and criticism will pour over you.'

England's summer trip to Brazil was to end in disappointment, not only for Williams but for the side and the country as a whole. Victory over Chile in the opening match in Rio de Janeiro was followed by one of the most inglorious defeats in English football history — 1-0 at the hands of no-hopers USA in Belo Horizonte. It was an unbelievable turn-up and, when Spain handed out a similar beating back in Rio three days later, England were booked on the first available plane home.

Wolves' fortunes the following season didn't do much to lift Williams out of any lingering Samba sadness, a disappointing final 14th place being compensated only by progress to a losing F.A. Cup semi-final against Newcastle. Williams, however, figured in high-scoring international victories against Northern Ireland and Wales in the autumn and again helped preserve England's unbeaten home record against foreign opposition when he made a fine save from Grumellon in the last 30 seconds of the 2-2 draw against France at Highbury 12 months later.

Although he continued to play at regular intervals for the Football League, Williams suffered a lengthy absence from the England side after playing against Wales at Cardiff two and a half weeks later on October 20, 1951. Injury cost him his place, Birmingham's Gil Merrick seizing his chance during an era that brought England their two infamous defeats against Hungary and another disappointing World Cup campaign in Switzerland in 1954.

'Losing my England place was the biggest disappointment of my career,' Williams said. 'I was injured before a Football League XI v Scottish League game and Gil came in and did very well. It was more than three years before I won any more full England caps. It's nice to have played 24 times for my country but I would like to have played a lot more.' Nevertheless, it's a haul of caps that had been beyond his wildest dreams a few years earlier when he represented the RAF in a game against Scotland. Seven goals rained in past the unfortunate youngster, the last of them from a Matt Busby penalty which Williams allowed to slither through his hands and over the line — despite being convinced the shot was deliberately mis-hit to give him a chance!

The match that finally brought him in from the international wilderness was the visit of West Germany on December 1, 1954. England won 3-1 and Williams was selected for five of the next six games as well, including the 1955 summer tour of France, Spain and Portugal. But his international farewell came on October 22 of that year, when he played his part in a 1-1 draw against the Welsh at Cardiff.

Back at Molineux, things had got worse before they got better, Wolves finishing 16th in 1951-52 and conceding their highest 'goals against' tally (73) since 1935-36. Williams played only 27 games out of a possible 45 in League and Cup and experienced a couple of the sort of injury setbacks he generally managed to avoid. 'The worst injuries I had were a snapped tendon in my shoulder and a bad kick on the calf,' he said. 'I was out for about 12 weeks and ten weeks respectively and they were serious setbacks.

'Generally, football was a more dangerous game in those days, especially for a goalkeeper. The boots were that much heavier and therefore a lot more painful when you went down at somebody's feet. Also, players were allowed to charge the keeper physically. Many's the time I've caught a cross and then been charged by a forward rushing in. It was a real art bouncing the ball and weaving out of the way of opponents. I remember once going to the cinema and seeing a Pathe News film clip of an England game against Wales. The Welsh centre-forward and I collided five times in the same incident before I managed to let go of the ball! I used to like to go out almost to the 18-yard line to take crosses but, once you had the ball, you could be pretty sure of getting thumped if you didn't let go of it quickly. Nat Lofthouse and I were great friends off the pitch but he used to dish out the rough stuff as much as anybody!

'Considering the protection keepers are given today,

Shouldering arms . . . From left: Billy Wright, Johnny Hancocks, Jesse Pye, Jimmy Dunn, Jimmy Mullen, Sammy Smyth, Bill Shorthouse, Billy Crook, Terry Springthorpe, Roy Pritchard, Laurie Kelly, Alf Crook, Bert Williams.

there's no real reason why they shouldn't carry on playing until the age of 45 — if they look after themselves. I think Neville Southall is probably the best in the world today but I'm a particularly big fan of Peter Shilton. He has been an example for any young lad to follow. Too many of the others are exhibitionists and showmen.

'I also think it's a myth that keepers have to be giants. At school, the biggest and toughest in the playground would always go in goal. But a good keeper should be able to more than double his length when he dives, so height isn't everything.'

Injury again took a large chunk out of Williams' 1952-53 contribution and Sims played 13 games as Wolves finished a close third behind Arsenal and Preston in the top three. But he reeled off another 100-plus League appearances over the next three seasons, Wolves winning the title for the first time in

1953-54, narrowly failing to retain it the following year and then finishing third.

Heady days, indeed — and nights! Floodlights had by now been installed at the famous old ground, the games against the likes of Honved, Moscow Dynamo and Spartak providing Williams with some of his happiest memories.

'Having missed out on playing for England against Hungary, it was great to face many of the same brilliant players at club level,' he added. 'People shouldn't forget that we won 3-2 in 1954 against a Honved side who included a lot of the players who had hammered England. It was a tremendous victory.

'There seemed to be as many people outside the ground that night as inside it. Thousands and thousands were locked out and had to make do with a running commentary relayed to them. But there wasn't a moment's trouble as far as I can remember. Afterwards, there were hats, scarves and even crutches that people had dropped in the crush and been unable to pick up. One lady even lost her shoes and our trainer, Joe Gardiner, had to lend her a pair of boots to go home in!

'One of the joys of playing then were the big crowds we had at home or away. We often travelled to an away game by train and ended up walking side by side with the crowds from the station to the ground. I can't imagine that happening today.'

Williams' own relationship with the crowds was almost legendary. As a goalkeeper, he seemed to possess an extra charisma in a team of stars and had two young admirers who often appeared at the players' tunnel when Wolves ran out for a home match. One would be dressed in old gold and black, the other in an emerald green keeper's jersey and they would have a sweet or good-luck charm with which to greet their hero. Williams used to take them by the hand, sometimes allowing them to carry his cap and gloves before bidding them farewell and leaving them to return to the crowd before kick-off. Imagine the surprise 30-odd years on when, a few months ago, one of those 'young admirers' — now with a young boy of his own — made himself known again during one of Bert's rare visits to Molineux.

By the start of the 1956-57 season, the 36-year-old Williams had decided it was time to set a retirement date for the following summer. Not that he had to, for he was still a credit to his profession, referred to by journalist Bob Ferrier in a series called 'Top Rung in Sport' in the most glowing of terms. Ferrier wrote: 'He's built like a middleweight champion, high-chested, clean-muscled and bursting with vitality. He moves with pantherish grace . . . and has the dignity of the perfect human. If the best type of footballer had to be immortalised in stone or on canvas, Williams would be the choice.'

The perfect sporting specimen or not, though, Williams was planning for the future. He had no wish to wait for others to tell him it was time to retire, nor did he want to drift from the football limelight into the pub business or anything similar. As much as he loved playing to the packed crowds of the day, he craved 'the good life' when he finally had to hang up the gloves. And, for him, that meant life in the country.

He made another 31 appearances for Wolves in 1956-57, helping the club to sixth place in the table but sharing in the humiliation of the notorious F.A. Cup defeat at home to Bournemouth in front of 42,011 disbelieving spectators on January 26. Finlayson, signed for £4,000 from Millwall at the start of the season, was pushing hard for a place and he was to become the new regular after Williams, at 37, had bowed out on something of a low note after successive away defeats against Portsmouth and Villa.

Within a few years, though, Williams could claim to have made as smooth a transition into business life as any living footballer. Never the restful type or the sort to spend his afternoons off wandering around the town-centre coffee bars, he found it easy to adapt to the longer working hours demanded in the business world.

Several years earlier, he had sown the seeds of his off-field success by inserting a notice in the window of a friend's tailor shop in Bilston. It read simply: 'Sports goods may be obtained within from Bert Williams.' His pulling power gave him a head start and the subsequent boom proved the old adage that, from little acorns, big oaks grow.

Eight months later, Williams had a shop of his own in Bilston and, the following year, opened a second, this time in Wolverhampton. His capacity for hard work, demonstrated in later years by the overlooking of family holidays and by the fact that he would spend many Sundays in only a dressing gown while attending to his book-keeping, brought rich rewards.

He was given an Arab gelding racehorse and duly acquired his dream home in the Shropshire countryside. He named the house 'Corcovado' after a magnificent granite figure of Jesus Christ he and his England team-mates had been lucky enough to see in 1950 on their climb to a Rio de Janeiro mountain-top. Williams had also converted an old Bilston vicarage into a sports centre at which three indoor cricket wickets were laid. His pride in having provided a facility to entice the local youngsters off the streets was compounded by a summer goalkeeper coaching class which produced, among others, Geoff Crudgington and West Ham's former Walsall and Queen's Park Rangers star Phil Parkes.

Today, well into his 71st year and with his business empire greatly expanded, his sporting interests centre largely on going shooting with his two sons. But, despite a fantastic success story in and out of the game, there are regrets. 'In retrospect, I should have carried on playing for another five years,' he says. 'I was certainly fit enough but I decided to pursue another career while I was still young and active. What is gratifying, though, is the recognition I still receive from football people more than 30 years after retiring from the game. I wonder how many of today's players will still be recognised in 30 years' time.'

FULL INTERNATIONAL CAPS (24)
(England score given first in each case)

1949: France (Paris) 3-1; Eire (Everton) 0-2; Wales (Cardiff) 4-1; Italy (Tottenham) 2-0.

1950: Scotland (Hampden) 1-0; Portugal (Lisbon) 5-3; Belgium (Brussels) 4-1; Chile (Rio de Janeiro) 2-0; USA (Belo Horizonte) 0-1; Spain (Rio de Janeiro) 0-1; Northern Ireland (Belfast) 4-1; Wales (Sunderland) 4-2; Yugoslavia (Arsenal) 2-2.

1951: Scotland (Wembley) 2-3; Argentina (Wembley) 2-1; Portugal (Everton) 5-2; France (Arsenal) 2-2; Wales (Cardiff) 1-1.

1954: West Germany (Wembley) 3-1.

1955: Scotland (Wembley) 7-2; France (Paris) 0-1; Spain (Madrid) 1-1; Portugal (Oporto) 1-3; Wales (Cardiff) 1-1.

CHAPTER 7

Peter Broadbent

'I ONLY SAW A FEW MINUTES OF ANYTHING OUT of the ordinary from him — and it was enough.' That is Stan Cullis's recollection of the scouting trip which was to lead him to the capture of Peter Broadbent in 1951.

And what a vital capture it was! The capture of an inside-forward who was to help Wolverhampton Wanderers to three League championship triumphs, one F.A. Cup success and on to their proud perch as pioneers of floodlit football.

There were seven full England caps along the way, too, to go alongside the 497 appearances and 145 goals he accumulated for Wolves. It was a phenomenal success-splashed career and one which, in terms of loyalty, was typical of the club at the time — and of football in general. In post-war England, footballers had neither the opportunity nor the inclination to chop and change clubs as they do today.

Broadbent, born in Elvington, Kent, moved north to the Midlands via a stop-off with one of London's less glamorous clubs, Brentford, and played for Shrewsbury Town, Aston Villa and Stockport County at the end of his career. But, in between, he served Wolves for no fewer than 14 seasons.

'There didn't seem any point in thinking about transfers all the while in those days,' he said. 'There weren't the same financial incentives for moving. In fact, the thing that deterred a lot of players from moving was knowing that they would

'You must be Peter Broadbent' . . . the nervous newcomer receives a welcoming handshake from his manager on day one.

have to move house as well. I was lucky because when I did eventually leave Wolves, we didn't have to leave our home at Codsall.

'Obviously, if I had played my football 20 years or so later, I would have made a lot more money out of the game. But I don't think I would swap the glory and the memories that came with playing for Wolves at that time. I don't think I could have served a finer club — nor at a better time.'

So what were the attributes that persuaded the most famous manager in Wolves' history to part from the club's tradition of producing their own players and splash out good money instead on one of somebody else's discoveries?

'He was a natural,' Cullis replied. 'There was a certain flair about his play and he did things spontaneously. His control and ability to go past players were his real hallmarks and he had a natural body-swerve which only comes to the really gifted players.'

It was an opinion which was to be shared by tens of

thousands of Wolves fans over the years and by hundreds of thousands of admirers nationwide and across the rest of Europe. A buzz would go round the ground when the ball arrived at his twinkling feet. A feeling of anticipation that something was going to happen. A real crowd favourite — that was Peter Broadbent. And it was noticeable when the players from the club's vintage years were paraded at Molineux before the nostalgic friendly against Moscow Dynamo just over a year ago, that nobody received a bigger cheer than he did.

Back in 1950-51, though, Cullis wasn't the only man to spot the potential of one of Britain's brightest young players. Newcastle United also eyed him eagerly at the start of a decade in which they went on to win the F.A. Cup three times. Brentford, Broadbent's first Football League club, realised they had a talent worth cherishing and held out for a fee approaching £10,000 — by no means a pittance four decades ago — when Wolves made their decisive and successful move for him.

The West London club's faith in the teenage star, in fact, had been demonstrated by the lengths to which they themselves had gone when they signed him from non-League Dover in May, 1950. Broadbent, 16 at the time, had agreed to sign professional at Griffin Park as soon as he turned 17 — and recalls: 'Two days before my birthday, I was playing at Margate in the final of something like the Kent Senior Cup. Brentford were so frightened that I was going to change my mind and sign for some other club that they had a taxi waiting outside the ground for me at the final whistle. They whisked me off and I stayed at the home of one of the scouting staff for two nights before I signed!'

Broadbent was in the Brentford first team within weeks, making the first of 16 League appearances in a side managed by Jackie Gibbons, a former Spurs player and England amateur international, and including 1980s England manager Ron Greenwood at centre half. But it wasn't long before Newcastle and Wolves became interested in him.

Goal-maker . . . Broadbent squares and Dennis Wilshaw scores against Newcastle United in the latter stages of the 1953-54 title triumph.

'Without me knowing, Stan Cullis went to watch me in one game and I think he sent his chief scout, George Noakes, to have a look at me in another at Leeds. John Charles, one of my heroes, was playing for Leeds, though, and I was too preoccupied with watching him to wonder who might be in the stand.

'The chap I remember being involved in the discussions with was a businessman called Cadwallader. He seemed to have contacts at all the big clubs and obviously liked Wolves. He talked me into going up to Wolverhampton on the train with my Mom and Dad and I was booked into one of the town's hotels overnight. Stan Cullis, George Noakes and Jack Howley, the secretary, were there to meet me and I didn't take much persuading to sign for them the next day.

'I think the fee was a record for a 17-year-old and it was a big step for me to take, considering I was so far from home. But it was a move I never regretted.'

Another big influence in Broadbent's move away from his native south-east was George Poyser, his manager at Dover, his coach at Brentford and, a short while later, his coach and landlord at Wolves! Within a few months of Broadbent's arrival at the club, Poyser made the same move, his family providing homely digs for the young player only a few yards from the main Molineux entrances in Waterloo Road.

Broadbent's signing, on February 22, 1951, was followed within days by his first appearance for Wolves reserves, and such was his early impact that he made his first-team debut less than a month later. The visitors to and victors at muddy Molineux that Saturday afternoon were Portsmouth, who were to play quite a significant part in his development as a cultured member of the truly great Wolves sides. Pompey also provided the opposition when he scored his only Football League hat-trick — this time in a 5-3 Boxing Day win at Fratton Park in 1958-59, the day before Wolves won 7-0 in the return meeting of the clubs.

Broadbent was actually on the losing side in his first eight games in Cullis's first team — an extraordinary statistic considering Wolves had been doing well in the League and had also reached and lost the semi-final of the F.A. Cup in the weeks prior to his breakthrough! Even the match which broke the run was less than memorable — a 0-0 end-of-season draw at Sunderland.

The early months of Broadbent's professional career had given little indication of the riches to come. The talent was there all right but few would have guessed he was going to emerge as a prolific goalscorer as well as a high-class provider.

He had scored only once in his 16 League games for Brentford and managed only the same number in his nine games for Wolves before the end of the 1950-51 season, breaking his duck in an exciting 3-2 defeat at Albion in the April.

But there was a possible reason for his slow start. As a lad, he had been a chronic hay fever sufferer and the specialised training he was put through at Molineux revealed a definite weakness. 'We could tell he had a chest problem, so we sent him off to the specialist to be checked over,' Cullis said. 'Fitness was a very important ingredient in our success and it was vital his weakness was identified and overcome.'

Goal-scorer . . . Broadbent starts the celebrations as the ball slithers through the St. Andrew's mud in a game against Birmingham City in 1963.

Broadbent's 18th birthday was celebrated in, of all places, South Africa, where a surprise party was thrown in his honour during Wolves' 1951 visit. But his Molineux career was to take another detour before it could really be said to be on the right track. Military service was still a way of life for the young men of post-war Britain and Broadbent's posting — confirmed on his return from playing against the likes of Natal, Southern Transvaal and Frontier State — was with the RAF, first to Padgate and then to Bridgnorth.

Physical training was very much part of his new life in uniform but Wolves saw less and less of him, apart from on match-days. 'In a football sense, it was two years of my life wasted,' he says. 'I played matches for the RAF, of course, and played with or against some pretty good players, like Jackie Mudie and John Charles. I also did plenty of training with them but I didn't do much training with Wolves and at times I only came back to Molineux for games.'

In the following 1951-52 season, Broadbent maintained his modest scoring record with one goal in 16 League appearances — and again his lucky club, Portsmouth, were on the receiving end. He also found the net in a 2-2 F.A. Cup third-round draw at Manchester City but it wasn't until after

Christmas that he was able to establish himself in a side struggling well below half-way in the First Division.

And it wasn't until the 1952-53 campaign that he became a regular in Cullis's side. He missed the opening-day victory over Cardiff but lined up at No. 10 in the next eight games and then switched to inside-right for 16 of the next 17. After two poor seasons, Wolves were doing battle again at the right end of the table and Broadbent played his part with five goals by the turn of the year. But the 5-3 defeat at Arsenal on January 17 was his first-team swansong for the season as he fell out of favour for the only time in his Wolves career.

Wolves went on to finish third, three points behind both champions Arsenal and runners-up Preston, their return to health being confirmed by the winning of the Central League title for the third successive season and by being runners-up in the F.A. Youth Cup.

For player and club, everything came right in 1953-54. Wolves won the Football League and Broadbent played 36 of the 42 games, scoring 12 goals in the process. With the likes of Sammy Smyth, Jimmy Dunn and Jesse Pye by now committed to the Molineux history books, Broadbent had made the inside-right shirt his own, forming an outstanding partnership with Johnny Hancocks, whose tally of 24 League goals was two behind Dennis Wilshaw's and matched by Roy Swinbourne's. A curious footnote to the season of triumph, though, was that Wolves' 96 League goals were shared among only seven players, Bill Slater being the only non-forward to find the net.

'It was a great season for me and the club,' Broadbent recalls. 'I suppose I had been signed as an eventual replacement for people like Jesse Pye, who was one of the best players I have ever seen, Sammy Smyth and Jimmy Dunn. Johnny Walker was another rival in my early days but I became a fixture in the side in the season we won the League and I was determined I was going to take some shifting.'

Wolves were within four points of retaining the title 12

Pick that one out, Gordon . . . Broadbent on target with a low drive that flashes past the great Gordon Banks during Wolves' 2-1 win at Leicester City in the 1959-60 F.A. Cup quarter-final.

months later, their shaky run-in of four defeats in eight games leaving them as runners-up and Chelsea as champions instead. Broadbent reeled off a further 38 League appearances, plus four in the F.A. Cup and one in the 4-4 Charity Shield draw with Albion, his only major disappointment being that he totalled only five goals.

But 1955-56 was to provide another breakthrough for him as Wolves were pipped for runners-up spot behind Manchester United and Blackpool. The scoring touch started to come back — ten goals in 39 League outings — and there was the bonus of further international recognition on top of the England Under-23 cap he had won against Italy two seasons earlier. This time he was called up for the England B side against Scotland.

A new right-sided partner came on the scene in 1956-57, £20,000 former West Ham winger Harry Hooper taking over from Hancocks. And in his one-season stay at the club, he and

Broadbent formed an effective combination, scoring 19 and 17 goals respectively to help Wolves to a final placing of sixth. Broadbent's tally, bolstered by another F.A. Cup goal, was highlighted by a brace in a 3-0 home win over Villa in the last game of the season. The previous day, Wolves had crashed 4-0 at Villa Park!

Broadbent was to slip from second to third in the Wolves scoring charts the following season but he was by no means disappointed. His 21 goals, including four in the Cup, were a vital back-up to those of Jimmy Murray (32) and Norman Deeley (23) and Wolves were champions for the second time in five seasons. For Broadent, came the additional satisfaction of a goalscoring appearance for the Football League side against the League of Ireland and, more importantly, his first full England cap.

It was no ordinary international either, but a World Cup group play-off game against the USSR in Gothenburg during the 1958 finals in Sweden. Sadly, though, England — despite the additional Wolves representation provided by Billy Wright and Bill Slater (Eddie Clamp also played earlier in the tournament) — lost 1-0 and were soon on their way home. It was their last game for nearly four months but Broadbent kept his place for the 3-3 draw away to Northern Ireland and had the pleasure of lining up in the same team as his mentor, Tom Finney.

Broadbent was absent when partial revenge, in the form of a 5-0 victory, was gained over the visiting Russians at Wembley in late October, 1958, but he was back a month later to delight West Midlands spectators with both goals in England's 2-2 draw with Wales at a vibrant Villa Park. 'It was a bit ironic that I should score the goals because I was playing schemer behind Nat Lofthouse. He was meant to score them but the chances obviously fell my way!

'I kept my place for the home games against Scotland and Italy later in the season and went on the summer tour of South America, when I only played in the opening game. That was

What all the fuss is about . . . Broadbent with the Football League championship trophy.

against Brazil in Rio de Janeiro and what a match it was! We lost 2-0 but I will remember the game for the size of the crowd — something like 130,000 and hardly an Englishman in it! We went on to Peru, Mexico and Los Angeles but I lost my place to Jimmy Greaves and didn't play again on the trip.

'Walter Winterbottom was manager and had an unusual way of letting you know if you were out of favour. The planes used to have first and second-class compartments and you knew you were out of favour if Walter asked you to sit in the cheaper seats! It was so obvious and the players used to have a good laugh about it.'

In the summer of 1959, however, Broadbent did have something with which to soften the blow of temporary rejection by England — a third championship medal. Just before the national side jetted off to the sunshine in early May, Wolves had confirmed their standing as the finest side in the country by retaining their title in magnificent fashion. Their winning margin over a Manchester United side rebuilt after the Munich air disaster was an emphatic six points and Broadbent — switched with great effect to inside-left for the second half of the season — played his part with 20 goals in his 40 League appearances. With continental competition now on the itinerary as well, he added two more goals in the home leg of the European Cup tie against Schalke 04 but Wolves' fleeting interest ended with a narrow defeat in West Germany.

So Broadbent had three championship winners' medals and six full England caps — the latter collection being increased by playing in the draw against Scotland at Hampden Park a few months later on April 19, 1960. But the prize and occasion that was to give him most pleasure throughout his long career was still a matter of weeks away. Wolves, with Broadbent scoring in the home and away legs of their preliminary round tie against Vorwaerts, went out of Europe at the hands of mighty Barcelona at the third hurdle and their grip on the title was to end in the heartbreaking disappointment of being runners-up to Burnley. But one more avenue to silverware remained open.

Wolves were still in the F.A. Cup, beating Newcastle United after a replay, Charlton Athletic, Luton Town and Leicester City on their way to the semi-final. Neighbours Villa then succumbed in a tight, tense showdown at neutral West Bromwich, leaving Wolves and Blackburn Rovers to battle it out in the final at Wembley on May 7.

'I had got married in 1956 and my wife Shirley was about eight months pregnant when the players set off for London on the Thursday night,' he says. 'The Cup final was virtually the only chance the wives had of enjoying a day out with the club and she had to miss it! I was ringing home every few hours but she managed to watch the game on TV at home because our son Gary didn't arrive until a few weeks later.

Wolves star graduates for England . . . Broadbent flies high in the 1-0 Wembley victory over Scotland in 1959 — his fourth full cap.

'There always seemed to be drama surrounding Cup finals. Derek Dougan, then a Blackburn player, put a transfer request in on the day of the game and their full-back, Whelan, broke his leg in the early stages. That made our task easier because there were no substitutes. My big mate, Norman Deeley, scored two of the goals and helped bring about an own goal as we won 3-0.

'It was the highlight of my Wolves career. The floodlit matches were tremendous and it was fantastic to win the League three times. But the championship was over eight or nine months. The Cup final was all about one afternoon and it was an unbelievable thrill to be part of a winning team at Wembley. As a manager, Stan Cullis was a disciplinarian and somebody we were frightened to be seen having a drink in front of. But we all let our hair down a bit at the banquet that night!'

In terms of England caps and major honours, it was the end of the line for the then 26-year-old Peter Broadbent. He reeled off another 141 League appearances for Wolves and rattled in a further 25 First Division goals. He was still one of Britain's most gifted footballers and continued to prove, over and over, what a bargain buy he had been more than a decade earlier. A place in Molineux's hall of fame is his forever and he remains sixth both in the club's all-time appearances and goals lists.

But Wolves were a club in decline and successive League finishes of 18th, 5th and 16th were not what their fans were used to. Cullis was sacked in September, 1964, and Broadbent, facing the prospect of reserve-team football under new manager Andy Beattie, left Molineux as well a few months later. His last goal was in a 2-1 home defeat by Leicester, his last first-team appearance in a 1-0 Boxing Day home defeat by Villa. Wolves' fans had seen the best and the last of one of their most talented players — some would say THE most talented.

Broadbent was sold to Shrewsbury for a then Gay Meadow record of £10,000 and had a successful 18 months before joining Villa for £7,500. But, true to their word, Wolves honoured him with a testimonial after he had left them. Such was his popularity that Derek Dougan, Don Howe, Jimmy Armfield, Bert Trautmann, Tom Finney and George Eastham turned out to play for an All Star XI for him at Molineux. And when the resulting cheque was being handed over at a sportsmen's evening at Wolverhampton's Victoria Hotel, then Molineux chairman John Ireland mourned: 'Wolves are losing a great soccer artist.'

At the end of the 1968-69 season, Broadbent left Villa and joined Stockport County on a free transfer, finally seeing out his playing days with non-League Bromsgrove Rovers.

With wife Shirley, he now owns a babywear shop in Halesowen High Street, having earlier run a grocery business nearer his home in the village of Codsall, just outside Wolverhampton. Despite the photographs and the scrapbook collection presented to him by his father just before the end of his career, he admits his recollection of many individual matches is hazy. Not surprising considering how many he played!

But he says: 'What I do remember are the battles I had with some of football's most famous players. One of my most memorable games was when we beat Spurs four or five at Molineux and Danny Blanchflower didn't know where he was at the final whistle! I also loved facing Len Shackleton, Raich Carter and Wilf Mannion. I was much younger then and they were the greats of the day.

'The trips abroad were also special, although I don't know how our wives stood it. We were away so long and so often. I think Wolves were the first British team to go to South Africa and Russia after the war and I was on both trips. We had one of our many laughs in Russia when we had the usual massage before one of the games. Not by a bloke, but by a 20st Russian woman who didn't speak a word of English. We had never seen a female in our dressing-room before!

'I also went to America, Canada and most of the European countries with Wolves and tours abroad were something you wanted to be involved with when you were younger. Often, I would come back from some trip and go straight off on a family holiday to Bournemouth or Cornwall. Once, I remember us going away with Norman Deeley and his wife. He was my big ally on and off the pitch.'

Broadbent, now 57 and suffering from an arthritic knee, doesn't watch much football these days. He prefers his golf and, as a former two-handicapper now playing off five, is largely responsible for having steered son Gary to a place on the European professional tour.

But it's for his grand five-club total of 629 League appearances (138 League goals) that he will be remembered. And for his sportsmanship. Peter Broadbent was never booked. He was a true gentleman and a true great.

FULL INTERNATIONAL CAPS (7)

(England score given first)

1958: USSR (Gothenburg) 0-1; Northern Ireland (Belfast) 3-3; Wales (Aston Villa) 2-2.
1959: Scotland (Wembley) 1-0; Italy (Wembley) 2-2; Brazil (Rio de Janeiro) 0-2.
1960: Scotland (Hampden) 1-1.

WOLVES APPEARANCES

League: 452. FA Cup: 31. European: 11. Charity Shield: 3. Total: 497. Goals: 145.

CHAPTER 8

Ron Flowers

TO SAY THAT RON FLOWERS WAS AN INSTANT hit for his country, would be as far off the mark as to say Wolverhampton Wanderers played intricate, complicated football in the 1950s. In fact, the forceful wing-half, who went on to assemble a proud collection of 49 full England caps, three League championship medals and an F.A. Cup winners' medal, thought his international career was doomed before it had really begun.

It was in May, 1955, in Paris's Colombes Stadium, that he pulled on a senior England jersey for the first time. And he played so badly that he feared it could also prove the last. He was left out of the side for the remaining two games of that summer tour and the wait to regain his place went on and on and on.

Thirty-two internationals and three and a half years elapsed before the next call came — and this time there were no squandered opportunities. Flowers, a striking blond Billy Wright lookalike, was there to stay for a good few years, during which he also took his tally of Wolves senior appearances towards a staggering final haul of 512. He was yet another of that famous Molineux breed of loyal, popular and immensely talented young men who inscribed the club's name on the world map.

By remaining at Wolves until 1967, he can truly be said to

have savoured the good times and also to have been around to wave them goodbye. He was the last playing link with the glory years — and the decline of a great club was well under way when he moved on at the age of 33. He had given Wolves most of his footballing life and, like so many of his earlier team-mates, had set the highest standards.

But it is Flowers' development and grooming, as well as his actual glorious career, that give an insight into Wolves' success at that time. He was born in the Yorkshire village of Edlington on July 28, 1934, the latest product of a football-mad family. His father had played at amateur level, his Uncle George had played professionally at nearby Doncaster Rovers and young Ronald had his sights on the same goal as he progressed via the Doncaster schools side.

Among his team-mates was inside-right Alan Finney — later to captain Sheffield Wednesday — and, together, they played in the Doncaster schools team who pulled off an unlikely 2-1 win against London Counties at Brentford. Flowers was given a shilling by his father whenever his team beat a good side — and there was another bob in it for him if he scored.

But the big prize — the chance to make his living from the game he loved — still awaited him. Sheffield Wednesday invited him to Hillsborough to discuss terms but he held fire, more intent on following family tradition and joining Doncaster. Almost inevitably, that chance came and the club of his dreams were also good enough to arrange a job for him in the nearby British Rail loco-sheds.

Strangely, though, they were less forward in giving him his chance on the field. He trained hard enough and thought his break would come. But he was allowed to drift away and instead play three times a week for the railway works side. Eventually, Doncaster allowed his registration to lapse without him kicking a ball in anger for them. Many times in subsequent years, they must have held their heads in shame!

Flowers went to play for a working men's club team and to

Flowers in bloom . . . the young product of Wath Wanderers, fresh-faced and determined.

attract the attention of Mark Crook, a 1930s Wolves winger who continued to play a big part in shaping the future of his former club. After retiring as a player, Crook bought a fish and chip shop in Yorkshire, where he also managed a side called Wath Wanderers in the village of Wath-on-Dearne, near Barnsley.

His plan was to cream off the area's best junior players, groom them for stardom and point them towards Molineux. The result was that a rich supply of promising teenagers was channelled towards Wolverhampton instead of towards the Sheffield clubs, Leeds or the North-East.

Wath, members of the Northern Intermediate League, even played in old gold and black and were one of the first clubs run specifically to produce players for a parent club. The policy paid off handsomely. Flowers signed for Wath at 16, made his debut in a game away to a Newcastle United youth side shortly afterwards and went with his team-mates that same afternoon to watch Wolves play Sunderland at Roker Park. In a subsequent match, he lost two teeth in a collision but still sported a big grin when later told of interest from Molineux.

Crook, who had originally fielded him at inside-right, saw him as the sort of powerful, attacking wing-half who had become synonymous with Wolves' success. The sort of player he could always remember the club having. Flowers and another Wath product, Dick Neal, were duly sent to the West Midlands for a trial, after which manager Stan Cullis offered both a professional contract. In Flowers' case, that amounted to £7 a week in the winter and £6 a week in the summer — a welcome development at a time when he was starting to dislike his job on the railways.

So, Flowers, a shy but proud young Yorkshireman, made the upheaval to ply his trade brilliantly in the West Midlands. But there was one more hitch before he was even measured up for a pair of boots. He and Neal agreed to meet at Sheffield Station on Monday, August 27, 1951, ready for the rail trip down to their new surroundings. It was only when they arrived in Wolverhampton that they realised it was the Tuesday that they were due on. Monday was Bank Holiday! Not having any digs for the night, Flowers stayed in Neal's lodgings and, while taking an exploratory walk round the town, bumped into Peter Broadbent, the lad with whom he was to share accommodation in the Chester Street home of a Mrs Long.

Once at the ground, the newcomer soon discovered his wasn't the only broad Yorkshire accent to be heard around the corridors of Molineux. Centre-forward Roy Swinbourne and full-back Jack Short, as well as Neal, were also Wath old boys and Joe Bonson, Ken Knighton, Peter Knowles and Barry Stobart were to arrive in the Black Country by the same route in later years.

The introductions of the starry-eyed 17-year-old to the seasoned professionals were performed by Jimmy Mullen and

Cap that . . . Ron Flowers with the last of his 49 England caps.

it wasn't long before Flowers made his club debut in the fourth team in a Worcestershire Combination game. Initial progress was rapid and he went on to be named as 12th man for the reserves' trip to Derby. But there were also familiar teething problems.

To put it starkly, he was becoming homesick and, with time on his hands and not enough to occupy it, he spent what he now considers to be too many evenings at dances and at the pictures. Sensibly, he found his own cure by devoting more time to training, often going back to the ground for extra work in the afternoons. On other occasions, he made a temporary switch of sports and developed a liking for golf — the game that takes much of his leisure time today.

Flowers was to grow six inches and put on two stone in his first 18 months at the club while goalkeeper Bert Williams taught him leg-stretching exercises that were to help improve his speed off the mark. The reward for his tenacity came two months after his Molineux arrival, in the form of promotion to the reserve side who had won the Central League in four of the previous five seasons.

But the lives of young professional footballers in post-war Britain faced one common obstacle — National Service — and Master Ronald Flowers became aircraftman second class 2569824 when he was kitted out at Padgate for the RAF two weeks before his 18th birthday. A few months later, in September, 1952, after being transferred to Hednesford, he was in his billet when a sergeant appeared demanding to know: 'Which one is Flowers? You'd better get down to Wolverhampton. You're playing in the League team against Blackpool on Saturday.'

The teenage hopeful was staggered, both by his call-up and by the RAF's cooperation in allowing him to play. 'I had played in a public practice match the previous Saturday and done quite well in the reserves, but it was still a shock to be in the first team so soon,' he said.

Sadly, there was to be no immediate success story. Flowers, handed the No. 5 shirt but then switched to left-half just before kick-off to leave the job of marking Stan Mortensen to Billy Wright, had an unhappy afternoon chasing the shadow of inside-forward Ernie Taylor. Blackpool were soon three up in front of a Molineux crowd of 48,598 and Flowers' debut goal — a powerful long-range header from a Johnny Hancocks corner just before half-time — was only temporary relief in a 5-2 defeat.

The new boy was withdrawn from the firing line for the win at Chelsea seven days later but he was back for the terrific 6-2 victory over Manchester United at Molineux. He made a further 18 League appearances that season and helped the club finish third in the table. Another 15 outings, but no goals, followed in Wolves' 1953-54 championship season and his steady progress turned to giant leaps forward 12 months later.

After being overlooked for the first three games, he came in to play 37 of the remaining 39 First Division matches, also appearing in four F.A. Cup ties and the Charity Shield draw against Albion. His arrival in League football was complete.

Flowers, 5ft 11ins and perfectly built, had also scored five goals in emerging as a powerful, attacking wing-half and his development was to lead to the happiest — and then possibly the saddest — two days of his career so far. He had already won England under-23 caps against Italy and Scotland that season, then, one morning in May, he was woken with a start.

He recalls: 'It was Peter Broadbent, my digs-mate, waving a *Daily Express* and telling me I was in the full England squad for the summer tour. Sixteen players had been named to go to France, Spain and Portugal and Roy Swinbourne convinced me afterwards that I would be receiving my first cap because I was the only right-half in the party. I was in among big names like Stanley Matthews, Don Revie, Roy Bentley and Nat Lofthouse — players I only really knew from the pictures I had collected from out of the old cigarette packets. It was a wonderful thrill to be included alongside them.'

Flowers, then 20, and Wolves team-mates Wright, Williams and Dennis Wilshaw, travelled by train to link up with their international colleagues at North London's Hendon Hall Hotel. And, sure enough, he did win his first cap on the day Wolves had four players in a national side for the first time. But it was anything but a joyous occasion and he was soon told in no uncertain terms that Matthews liked the ball played to his feet, NOT to run on to. By common consent, he had a shocker and couldn't wait for the final whistle to blow on England's 1-0 defeat.

There were consoling words from various quarters as he was restricted to a watching brief at the subsequent games in Madrid and Oporto. But perhaps the most telling comment came from journalist and former playing hero Charlie Buchan at the post-match banquet in Paris. He told the dejected newcomer: 'Don't worry, son. I've slated you but you're young enough to come back.'

Despite losing his place to Jimmy Dickinson, the

disappointment had partly worn off when Flowers returned home to Doncaster. And pride took over when he handed his first cap to his father and fulfilled the promise he had made to take his parents on holiday to Blackpool if ever he played a full international for England.

Not that there was much time for self-pity anyway, with the 1955-56 season fast approaching. But it was in that campaign that Flowers found the competition provided by Wright, Eddie Clamp and Bill Slater hot to handle — and he made only 19 League and cup appearances for third-placed Wolves. International recognition also passed him by and, to an extent, he found himself having to re-establish himself the following term.

He duly did that with 39 League appearances and two in the Cup, also facing the Irish League on his debut in the Football League side. The motto on the Molineux dressing-room wall, 'There's no substitute for hard work,' could have been thought up with him in mind, for he toiled away at building up his speed and also at improving his first touch. Wolves' system dictated that he should release the ball early to colleagues, rather than run with it.

Whatever criticism the London Press threw at the Cullis style, the results did the talking in 1957-58. Wolves won the title for the second time in five years, reached the quarter-final of the Cup as a bonus and their players made even greater inroads into the England set-up. The club were again well represented at the World Cup and Flowers, his spirits lifted by another Football League v Irish League outing, was under consideration for the senior side again late in 1958 after an absence of more than three years.

He had scored in each of the last two games of Wolves' championship triumph and had gone into the following season in fine heart. The title was destined to remain at Molineux, due in no small part to a 'goals for' tally of 110, and Wolves — already the pioneers of floodlit football and the scourge of Europe in the process — had the extra incentive of competing in continental competition for the first time.

Champions . . . Wolves 1957-58. Back row from left: Eddie Clamp, Jimmy Murray, Gerry Harris, Malcolm Finlayson, Bill Slater, Ron Flowers, Eddie Stuart. Front: Bobby Mason, Norman Deeley, Billy Wright, Stan Cullis, Peter Broadbent, Colin Booth, Jimmy Mullen.

As League champions, they were in the hat with the big boys for the European Cup — and it was their first-round trip to face the Germans of Schalke 04 in November that was to mark an important watershed in Flowers' career. Wolves actually fell at that hurdle, following up a 2-2 first-leg draw at Molineux with a battling 2-1 defeat in the return. But there was huge personal consolation for him.

'It was the best day of my life, more wonderful even than winning an F.A. Cup medal, when Stan Cullis came up to me and broke the news that I'd been recalled by the England selectors,' he added. 'We were training at the Düsseldorf Sportschule at the time and, after three and a half years out of the national side, I was absolutely delighted to be back. It was for the game against Wales at Villa Park, which had always been a lucky ground for me. It turned out to be a lucky ground for Peter Broadbent as well because he scored both our goals in a 2-2 draw.'

This time, Flowers came into full bloom. He played well enough to retain his place for the 1-0 win against Scotland at Wembley five months later, so experiencing his first playing trip to a stadium he had previously visited only when watching England beat then World Cup holders West Germany in 1954. Incredibly, he didn't miss any of the next 38 senior internationals. For a player who had flopped when given his first opportunity, a run of 40 successive appearances in the side was a quite brilliant follow-up.

'It was the summer of 1963 before I missed another full international,' he added. 'There were some memorable victories and tours in that time — experiences which provided me with more highlights in a few years than most people enjoy in a lifetime.

'A few days after I broke my nose in the 2-2 draw against Italy at Wembley, we went on a tour of Brazil, Peru, Mexico and USA in 1959 and I'll never forget playing at the Maracana Stadium in Rio de Janeiro. The sight of something like 180,000 fans, many letting off firecrackers, was just incredible. I swapped shirts with the Brazilian No. 6 at the end and consider his jersey one of my proudest possessions.

'At the end of the same tour, we played USA at the Los Angeles Dodgers baseball stadium. That was one of the worst international pitches I played on because it had a huge slope and was covered in dust. But we didn't mind too much. We won 8-1 and I was lucky enough to score twice. Playing at Hampden Park was something else I'll always remember because I discovered what tricks the wind could play with the ball when it howled round those massive stands.'

Having missed out on the 1958 World Cup finals, Flowers was determined to make it to Chile four years later. But there were problems en route. In the 3-3 home draw against Yugoslavia in May, 1960, he found himself pushed back so much that he was almost a second centre-half alongside Peter Swan. Manager Walter Winterbottom obviously liked the idea, though, because he told him to play there from the start in the match against Spain in Madrid a few days later. The new system was again retained despite a 3-0 defeat and, when Flowers was once more used in a defensive role in the 2-0 beating in Hungary the following week, he started to lose interest in playing for his country.

The new 4-2-4 line-up, with Bobby Robson and Johnny Haynes fulfilling the attacking midfield roles, was the talk of the Fleet Street sports writers — and so determined was Winterbottom to make it work that he arranged special practice matches against Manchester City and Burnley. The result was that England went to Belfast early the following season, won 5-2 against the Irish — and Flowers began enjoying international football again. But Cullis had to be on his guard when he welcomed him back to the Wolves fold after international duty. 'Don't forget you're playing for Wolves today, not England,' he would say. 'I want you getting forward, not playing in defence.'

Defensive or not, Flowers scored his third England goal in an 8-0 Wembley slaughter of Mexico in 1961, then, on the hottest afternoon he could ever recall playing football on, scored the equaliser against Portugal in Lisbon to secure qualification for the World Cup finals. Come the following summer, he hit another rich goal-scoring vein for his country, finding the net in five internationals out of six, mainly from the penalty spot.

'I scored against Austria and Switzerland at Wembley and then converted penalties in our first three games after we had gone out to South America for the World Cup,' he said. 'We left early to acclimatise and beat Peru 4-0 in Lima in a warm-up game in which Jimmy Greaves scored a hat-trick. But things weren't so straightforward when the tournament started.'

In the opening group game against Hungary in front of only 3,000 spectators in Rancagua, Flowers undid his earlier good work with the slip which brought about the Magyars' winning goal. He again scored from the spot as England recovered by beating Argentina 3-1, and progress to the next stage was assured thanks to a dreadful goalless draw against Bulgaria.

'It was then that we went out 3-1 to the eventual winners, Brazil, in Vina del Mar,' Flowers adds. 'But it was a great game and I remember coming home and thinking we could win the World Cup on home soil in 1966 . . .'

A lot of water had gone under the Molineux bridge in the meantime and would continue to do so before Sir Alf Ramsey and his players became the toast of the nation. Wolves, F.A. Cup winners in 1960, had had a second sortie into the European Cup in that same season, going out to Barcelona after impressively beating Vorwaerts and Red Star Belgrade.

But all was not well between Flowers and the club. After earlier denying that he wanted to leave Molineux, where he at times lost his place amid the fierce competition provided by Wright, Slater and Clamp, he found himself in a pay dispute in 1960. The lifting of the maximum wage had raised footballers' financial demands and Flowers thought he could provide a better future for wife Yvonne and his young family by moving on. But, after several difficult weeks in which his team-mates had joked 'Here comes the rebel' when he reported for pre-season training, agreement was reached with chairman Jim Baker. His bonuses now amounted to £4 for a win, £2 for a draw and £60 for an England cap, with £2 a day expenses when he was on international duty.

He repaid the faith shown in him by making 36 League appearances in Wolves' surge to third place in 1960-61, plus another three in a European Cup Winners' Cup run that ended against Glasgow Rangers in the semi-final, but the following season was one best forgotten. Wolves flopped to a final placing of 18th, went out of the Cup at home to Albion and suffered two more body blows with the departures of Slater and South African-born full-back Eddie Stuart. The latter outgoing, however, led to Flowers being named club captain on July 17, 1962, after agreeing another two-year contract.

His 300th League game followed a few weeks later against

Flowers farewell . . . departing from centre stage at the end of his playing career, accompanied by FIFA referee Jack Taylor.

Blackburn Rovers and, 11 years after leaving his native Yorkshire, he was also about to emulate the feat of Cullis, Wright and Slater in captaining country as well as club. Following a brief absence from the national side, he was back for the 8-1 romp against Switzerland in Basle in June, 1963, and then returned from another few months in the wilderness to face Eire in Dublin and embark on a tour of USA and Brazil.

'I captained England a couple of times at the end but there was one more big surprise in store,' he says. 'I had played two games at the end of 1964 and another one against West Germany in Nuremberg in May, 1965. Then Sir Alf favoured Nobby Stiles and I thought my England days were over. It was the biggest shock of my life when he called me up for the World Cup finals! Why he picked me, I don't know. But I was delighted all the same. I knew I wasn't going to play a big part but, at 32 or 33, it was a bonus just to be involved.

'We had already had a get-together at Lilleshall and a tour of Finland, Norway, Denmark and Poland, when we arrived at the Hendon Hall Hotel in London. I shared a room with Jimmy Armfield and I remember turning to him on the bench during one of the tour games and saying I thought we would win the World Cup. I wasn't sure we would win every game but I couldn't see anyone beating us.'

As expected, Flowers wasn't called upon as England followed up an opening draw with Uruguay by beating Mexico and France in their other group games and then overcoming Argentina and Portugal. But he nearly made the grandest of entries into the tournament on the never-to-be-forgotten final day, July 30, 1966. 'I was cover for Jack Charlton and Bobby Moore and, on the night before the final against West Germany, big Jack went to bed early with a chill. Sir Alf pulled me to one side to say: "If he's not better in the morning, you'll be in."

'But he was all right and I watched the drama unfold from the stand — or at least most of it. I was with Jimmy Greaves, John Connelly, Ron Springett, Peter Bonetti, Gerry Byrne, Norman Hunter, Terry Paine, Ian Callaghan and George Eastham — players, like me, in the squad but on the sidelines. Sir Alf had fixed it that, if we were winning, we were to be allowed out of the stand and down to the bench two or three minutes from the end, to be ready to go on to the pitch for the celebrations.

'We were 2-1 up when we got up from our seats but, while in the lift, we heard a roar and a lot of groans — and realised the Germans had equalised! But we saw the two goals Geoff Hurst got to complete his hat-trick in extra-time and we joined in the celebrations after all. It was a magnificent occasion and a magnificent weekend.

'People have asked me since whether I felt left out with not playing. But I never looked at it that way because I had never expected to be involved in the first place. And Sir Alf had the knack of making you feel part of everything. When my England career was over, he said I was welcome to go and watch any matches I wanted and could even have a pre-match meal and travel on the team coach if I wished. Not that I ever took him up on the offer.'

Not surprisingly, after such heights, the rest of Flowers' career was an anti-climax. He went on to complete a League and cup tally of 512 games (37 goals), leaving him behind only Derek Parkin (609), Kenny Hibbitt (574) and Billy Wright (541). But Wolves had been relegated in 1964-65 for the first time in 42 seasons and Flowers, troubled by a back injury, played only a small part as they returned to the First Division at the second attempt. He moved on in 1967 to spend two seasons at Northampton Town but the old sharpness had gone. He returned to the West Midlands to play for non-league Telford United, whom he led to Wembley twice as acting manager before leaving football to concentrate on the Wolverhampton sports shop he still runs.

His injury, diagnosed as disc trouble, brought the curtain down somewhat sadly on a tremendous career that had also brought him 13 appearances for the Football League and seven unofficial England outings. To his own surprise, he had outstayed Cullis at Molineux, the greatest manager in Wolves history being sacked early in 1964-65. 'Stan was like the South Bank,' he added. 'I thought he would be there forever. It was a huge shock when we read in the papers that he was going.'

Flowers' own magnificent service was rewarded by a belated 1971 testimonial watched by 21,000 fans. The only people to derive any satisfaction from his retirement were the rival wing-halves and inside-forwards whose jobs he made so difficult for 17 years. When it came to Flowers, they received no bouquets whatsoever.

FULL INTERNATIONAL CAPS (49)

(England score given first)

1955: France (Paris) 0-1.

1958: Wales (Aston Villa) 2-2.

1959: Scotland (Wembley) 1-0; Italy (Wembley) 2-2; Brazil (Rio de Janeiro) 0-2; Peru (Lima) 1-4; Mexico (Mexico City) 1-2; USA (Los Angeles) 8-1: Wales (Cardiff) 1-1; Sweden (Wembley) 2-3; Northern Ireland (Wembley) 2-1.

1960: Scotland (Hampden) 1-1; Yugoslavia (Wembley) 3-3; Spain (Madrid) 0-3; Hungary (Budapest) 0-2; Northern Ireland (Belfast) 5-2; Luxemborg (Luxembourg) 9-0; Spain (Wembley) 4-2; Wales (Wembley) 5-1.

1961: Scotland (Wembley) 9-3; Mexico (Wembley) 8-0; Portugal (Lisbon) 1-1; Italy (Rome) 3-2; Austria (Vienna) 1-3; Luxemborg (Arsenal) 4-1; Wales (Cardiff) 1-1; Portugal (Wembley) 2-0; Northern Ireland (Wembley) 1-1.

1962: Austria (Wembley) 3-1; Scotland (Hampden) 0-2; Switzerland (Wembley) 3-1; Peru (Lima) 4-0; Hungary (Rancagua) 1-2; Argentina (Rancagua) 3-1; Bulgaria (Rancagua) 0-0; Brazil (Vina del Mar) 1-3; France (Sheffield Wednesday) 1-1; Northern Ireland (Belfast) 3-1; Wales (Wembley) 4-0.

1963: France (Paris) 2-5; Scotland (Wembley) 1-2; Switzerland (Basle) 8-1.

1964: Eire (Dublin) 3-1; USA (New York) 10-0; Portugal (Sao Paulo) 1-1; Wales (Wembley) 2-1; Holland (Amsterdam) 1-1.

1965: West Germany (Nuremberg) 1-0.

1966: Norway (Oslo) 6-1.

WOLVES APPEARANCES

League: 467. F.A. Cup: 31. European: 11. Charity Shield: 3. Total: 512. Goals: 37.

CHAPTER 9

Bill Slater

THE SAME POLITENESS WITH WHICH BILL Slater helped make his name in and out of football cut no ice with Stan Cullis the day they first met.

Slater, a tall lean young man who had already played in an F.A. Cup final for Blackpool, had no great ambitions in the game when he knocked on the manager's door at Molineux in the summer of 1952. In his hand, he clutched a letter of introduction from Brentford, for whom he had turned out the previous season. With new bride Marion, he was moving to the Midlands to take up a teaching post at Birmingham University, determined to continue his football only in an amateur capacity.

Cullis read the letter, which was initiated by the same businessman who had set up Peter Broadbent's move from Brentford to Wolves a couple of years earlier. Then he sighed and said: 'Very interesting.' Not wishing to appear too pushy, Slater said: 'I am not too bothered which team I play in as long as I'm given a regular game.' It was a remark that didn't impress Cullis. 'Young man,' he replied, 'I'm not interested in anyone who doesn't want to play in the first team.'

For the intelligent 25-year-old, it was an immediate insight into the thinking of the man who made Wolverhampton Wanderers great. But the uneasy 'getting to know you' exercise was soon forgotten. Cullis, already well aware of Slater's ability as a wing-half, signed him on the spot and proceeded to steer him through a Molineux career of 339 first-team appearances, many of them as skipper. In 11 glorious years, the newcomer who 'just wanted a regular game' won three League championship medals, an F.A. Cup winners' medal and 12 full England caps.

Before and during his Wolves career, he also picked up 21 England amateur caps, representing his country both in the 1952 Olympic Games in Helsinki and in the 1958 World Cup finals in Sweden. But, despite emerging as an elegant and commanding centre-half of true international quality, he remained reluctant to commit himself fully to the game. Even when he turned professional in 1954, it was only on a part-time basis, his availability for Wolves being restricted by his teaching duties, particularly when it came to night matches and end-of-season tours.

In short, he never wanted to turn his back on the rewarding life he had cultivated outside the game. And, when the time came for him to blow the whistle on his playing days, he threw himself head-first into a multitude of new jobs and posts, such as deputy director of Crystal Palace sports centre, director of physical education at Liverpool and Birmingham universities, chairman of the West Midlands Sports Council and president of the British Amateur Gymnastics Association. Such devotion to sport inevitably brought the ultimate reward and it was the proudest day of William John Slater's life when he was summoned to Buckingham Palace in 1982 to receive the OBE from the Queen.

Now 63, retired and living a few miles west of Wembley, Slater is still active in the gymnastic circles in which his daughter Barbara won fame — and a place in the 1976 Montreal Olympics — before branching out into a career in television.

The story of his success is certainly an unusual one. He was born at Clitheroe, near Blackburn, on April 29, 1927, and decided at an early age that he wanted to be a teacher. But his

Captain cool . . . Slater leads Wolves out before their 5-1 slaughter of Chelsea at Stamford Bridge at the end of the 1959-60 season. Slater, followed by Malcolm Finlayson and Gerry Harris, led the side to F.A. Cup final glory at Wembley the following week.

football skills caught the eye of the local scouts and, after playing for the Army in West Germany's Rhineland during his three years in the Physical Training Corps, he progressed towards Football League status. Having played in the Lancashire and District Youth League, he joined one of the county's biggest clubs, Blackpool, in 1944.

As was to be the case throughout his career, his

availability was limited by other demands — at that time a physical education course he was taking at college in Leeds. 'I just played for Blackpool as often and as best as I could,' Slater recalls. 'It was far from an ideal arrangement because often I would set off for home matches at 11 or 11.30 a.m. after a couple of hours in the gym. More than once, I started games feeling weary, so Blackpool were keen for me to turn professional. But I didn't want that.

'While I was with them, though, I was lucky enough to play in the 1951 F.A. Cup final against Newcastle. I wasn't in the side round the time of the semi-final but Alan Brown broke his leg shortly afterwards and that gave me my chance. We lost 2-0 to a couple of goals from Jackie Milburn but it was tremendous, particularly as an amateur, just to be involved.

'Unfortunately, I had to be back in Leeds that night and was on a train packed with celebrating Newcastle supporters when the rest of the Blackpool players were gathering for the customary banquet. It was some journey, all of which I spent sitting in a corner and hiding my face in case I was recognised as a member of the opposition camp!'

After 30 League games and nine goals for Blackpool, he moved to Brentford in 1951. His college course was at an end and the move to West London meant he was closer to girlfriend Marion, whom he married a few months later. Griffin Park was seen very much as a brief stopping-off point, though, as Slater was to take up a teaching post at Birmingham University in the next year. But his brief stint of seven League matches did pitch him into a distinguished half-back line also containing Jimmy Hill and Ron Greenwood.

He was still fully amateur but the loyalties he divided between football and teacher-training brought more than just a few logistic problems. On the plus side, he also received early recognition from his country, the first of his England amateur caps coming in 1952. In the same year, he took part in the football tournament in the Helsinki Olympics and showed the academic side to his nature on his return.

Running round Wembley with the Cup . . . Slater receives a helping hand from right-half Eddie Clamp as Wolves embark on their lap of honour in 1960. Norman Deeley leads the rest of the happy band.

'Hungary won the gold medal and I was so impressed by them that I came home and wrote an article for the Football Association magazine, *F.A. News*,' he said. 'They had some really great players but I don't think many people took much notice of what I said. They seemed to think the Hungary side weren't the real thing because all the players were amateur. But a few months later, they went to Wembley and hammered England 6-3!'

By the time of the Magyar invasion, Slater was becoming established at Molineux, his close-season move in 1952 being completed despite the reservations of two directors, who were unhappy at an amateur being signed by a big First Division club. He was a rare breed indeed. He received no wage at Molineux — only reimbursement of the expenses incurred by his train trips to and from home in Bournville, Birmingham.

'The club were good to me, though, because they used to single me out and give me a turkey or something similar as a

Christmas present. And the players were kind. They used to buy me a gift as well and I had a clock one year. Training was a problem, though, because my commitments at the university meant they hardly saw me at Wolves between matches. And I also arrived at a time when there was a lot of competition for wing-half places from players like Billy Crook, Ron Flowers, Bill Baxter and Billy Wright.'

Nevertheless, he soon forced his way into Cullis's all-star team. His League debut for Wolves came at left-half in a magnificent 6-2 win over Manchester United at Molineux on October 4, 1952, and he went on to play another 16 games in a season which ended with a pleasing final placing of third. The three goals he scored, one of them while wearing the No. 10 shirt in a 3-2 pre-Christmas win at Sheffield Wednesday, also showed he retained a few of the instincts developed when playing at inside-left earlier in his career.

In Wolves' first championship-winning season, 1953-54, Slater was an even more vital cog, reeling off 39 League appearances and prompting his manager to hand him the No. 4 jersey no fewer than 36 times. Even the great Billy Wright couldn't claim to be such a regular fixture in any one position!

Slater's continued excellence inevitably led to Wolves wishing to secure a stronger hold on him — and they met with partial success in 1954. With the permission of Birmingham University, he turned part-time professional and, for his boldness, was rewarded with a princely signing-on fee of £10! The 6ft defender, who, in his earlier days, had struggled to gain his clearance for club games if they clashed with amateur internationals, was now close to a call-up for the full England side — and still a one-off at Molineux.

'The big problem was still combining teaching with playing and training, so a special clause had to go into my Wolves contract,' he added. 'I was okay for pre-season training and pre-season tours because they fell in the university holidays. But, when the two overlapped, university came first. I would never ask for time off to play in matches when I had lectures. And I couldn't go on end-of-season tours.

'Actually doing the training wasn't a problem, though, because I had an average of about 20 one-hour lectures a week and was left with plenty of free time. I obviously had a knowledge of the necessary training routines from my job and I would have been cheating only myself if I hadn't buckled down to some hard work in between my teaching duties. Not that I would have lasted long at Wolves if I hadn't been fit. I would soon have been found out!'

Slater, whose first game in the paid ranks was the 6-1 slaughter of Sheffield United in February, 1954, missed the 4-4 Charity Shield draw with Albion the following season for the aforementioned reason. But he had the considerable consolation less than two months later of making his senior England debut in the 3-2 victory over Wales at Wembley. He had well and truly arrived.

He kept his place at left-half in the more emphatic defeat of West Germany at the same venue three weeks later and, back at Molineux, had made the No. 4 jersey his personal property. As Wolves marched towards a final place of second behind Chelsea in the First Division, Slater slipped temporarily out of the international reckoning because of the emergence of Dudley's Duncan Edwards.

It was to be another three years before, in the wake of the Munich air disaster, Slater was back in the national side. The brilliant Edwards became one of the most-mourned of the casualties of Manchester United's ill-fated flight home from Belgrade on February 6, 1958 — and the England No. 6 shirt was vacant again in the most tragic circumstances.

'We were due to play at Manchester United the weekend after the crash but the game was obviously postponed,' Slater added. 'Instead, we all reported to Molineux to pay our respects to the victims. We went out on to the pitch in our everyday clothes and many thousands of fans turned up to join in the tribute. It was a very moving occasion. United were probably the only side to touch us at that time because Wolves were the nearest team to what Liverpool are today.'

The installation of floodlights at Molineux in the mid-1950s had increased Slater's availability for matches, the later kick-offs enabling him to travel across the West Midlands in good time to take his place in the side for home night games. He converted two penalties against Tottenham in the first League game under the Wolverhampton lights and played in the famous floodlit victories over the likes of Moscow Spartak and Honved. Like all his team-mates, he found them to be of 'special interest'.

But his fortunes looked like turning a little sour in 1957-58 as he found himself confined to Wolves' reserves for long spells. His first senior outing of the season came just before Christmas when he replaced the unwell Broadbent in the 2-0 home win over Everton and, when he switched to left-half to deputise for flu victim Ron Flowers in the Boxing Day clash at Tottenham, he was to share in Wolves' disappointment at losing for the first time in 19 matches.

Slater became a virtual regular in the second half of the season, though, and Wolves' prolonged success in the First Division kept him in the limelight. He was the man England turned to with the No. 6 shirt for the first post-Munich game, against Scotland at Hampden on April 19, 1958, his inclusion coming at considerable personal cost. England won 4-0 but Slater and club colleague Wright missed out on the celebrations back at Molineux on the afternoon that Wolves beat big rivals Preston North End 2-0 to lift the title for the second time.

Slater, though, who also missed the emotion-filled 4-0 win at Old Trafford two days later, was used to such clashes between club and country and was more than compensated by keeping his place for the next seven internationals. It proved a glorious end to the season for him because, as well as figuring in Wolves' championship success, he impressed sufficiently in the matches against Portugal, Yugoslavia and Russia to earn his ticket to the World Cup finals in Sweden.

There, he certainly wasn't short of good company and, in the opening group game against the Soviet side with whom

Every captain's dream . . . Slater is held aloft by Ron Flowers and Peter Broadbent as Wolves savour the glory of their 3-0 F.A. Cup final success over Blackburn Rovers. Completing the line-up are (back row from left) Gerry Harris, Malcolm Finlayson, Eddie Clamp, George Showell, Norman Deeley. Front: Barry Stobart, Des Horne, Jimmy Murray.

England had drawn 1-1 in Moscow three weeks earlier, he figured in an all-Wolves half-back line of Clamp, Wright, Slater! Broadbent made his bow later in the tournament but there was to be no happy ending. Draws against Russia (2-2), eventual winners Brazil (0-0) and Austria (2-2) left England facing a play-off with the Soviets and, with less than 48 hours to recharge the batteries, they lost 1-0 in Gothenburg.

Slater had played in all four games and said 'The World Cup was much smaller then than it is now and the one consolation we had was that we were the only side to draw or win against Brazil. But, overall, it was a disappointing tournament for us and we failed to progress past the first stage.'

Wright and Slater were present as revenge was duly gained the following autumn, Russia being crushed 5-0 at Wembley.

But both were to bow out of the international spotlight in quick succession in the next two years. Wright signed off on the 1959 summer tour of South America, Mexico and North America — though no-one was to know it until he announced his shock retirement at Molineux a few weeks later — and Slater's 12th and final cap came at No. 5 in the 1-1 draw against the Scots at Hampden Park on April 19, 1960.

In between the two England swansongs, Slater was duly promoted to Wolves skipper in succession to Wright and, like his predecessor, became a right-hand man to Cullis: a thinker, an inspiration, an example of everything good in the English game and a man for the manager to dicuss tactics and other club matters with on long coach and train journeys. He was also the latest in a long line of inspirational wing-halves and centre-halves who had skippered or were to skipper the club. Out of the same mould in later years came the likes of Ron Flowers, Mike Bailey, Emlyn Hughes and Alistair Robertson.

'It was unusual for a captain to be part-time,' Slater admits. 'But it was a great honour and privilege. As with my training arrangements, it didn't seem to matter too much because it seemed to work and we were successful. I still couldn't get away for some games, though, and I was disappointed to have to miss some of the ties when we went into European competition at the end of the 1950s. I remember, for example, coming back into the side for the home leg of the European Cup match against Barcelona in 1960 after missing the 4-0 defeat in the first leg in Spain. It was all over by the time I got involved in the tie!'

There was one particularly humorous aside to Slater's availability problems. For a vital end-of-season night game at Shefield United in 1955-56, he didn't have time to meet up with the rest of Wolves' squad, so two cars and a small aeroplane were laid on in an effort to get him from Birmingham University to Bramall Lane. But the master plan ended in failure.

'My wife rushed me from the university to Elmdon

Airport and there should have been plenty of time for me to get to the ground,' Slater recalls. 'It was a small two-seater plane that didn't fill me with a lot of confidence in the first place but the problems really started when we neared the end of the journey. The pilot had been told to look for the Lodge Moor airfield, where a car would be waiting to rush me away. But he hovered over the landing area for ages and then decided he was at the wrong place.

'Little did we know that the waiting car, with our scout George Noakes frantically waving a towel to try to attract our attention, was below us. We flew to an airfield at Worksop 20 miles away and, of course, there was no-one there to meet me! I ended up hitching a lift to Bramall Lane, arrived well into the game and got in through some open gates — just in time to see us throw away a 3-1 lead and draw 3-3. George Showell had taken my place and Stan Cullis was none too pleased at the chain of events.

'It wouldn't have been too bad but the draw cost us second place to Blackpool behind Manchester United in the final table and that meant quite a loss of money to the players. The maximum wage was still in operation and footballers looked to make a bit extra the higher they finished in the top five or six.'

With Wright fading into the club's golden past after retiring following Wolves' retention of the title in 1958-59, there was a gap to fill at No. 5, so Slater, like his predecessor, made the switch from wing-half to centre-half at about the time he was made captain.

The 1959-60 season didn't start in any blaze of glory for Slater because he initially flexed his muscles in the reserves, Clamp, Showell and Flowers forming the first-team half-back line. Even when he was recalled, it was in the inside-forward position he had occupied earlier in his career. He scored twice in a memorable 6-4 September 5 win at Manchester City and had to wait another three weeks to be given his old wing-half role — this time against a Blackburn Rovers side who were to play a significant part in Wolves' season.

But, after South African Eddie Stuart had been given a few games at centre-half and Showell had been injured in the Boxing Day defeat at Bolton Wanderers, Slater was handed the jersey — and made it his own. With the exception of the European Cup game in Barcelona in February, he was an ever-present at No. 5 for the rest of the season, Wolves finishing a close runner-up to Burnley in the championship race. Glory came instead in the F.A. Cup.

After progressing past the fourth round only once in the previous four seasons, Wolves suddenly rediscovered the knockout touch. They overcame Newcastle in a third-round replay, edged out Charlton Athletic in round four and sent Luton Town packing 4-1 at Kenilworth Road at the next stage. Leicester City, fellow finalists in 1949, were next to bite the dust — beaten 2-1 at Filbert Street — and neighbours Aston Villa were pipped 1-0 in a tense semi-final at the packed Hawthorns. So Wolves were through to the final against Blackburn and a McGrath own goal, together with a brace by winger Norman Deeley, secured a comprehensive 3-0 win in front of a 98,776 crowd.

Slater, who started the season in the reserves, had ended it as captain of a winning side at Wembley — and the headline 'It's Ours Again' screamed out of the front page of Wolverhampton's *Sporting Star*. 'It was a glorious occasion,' Slater says. 'The League achievements were probably greater but the F.A. Cup final is always a highlight. It was great to be a winner after being a loser with Blackpool nine years earlier.'

Remarkably, for a player who had missed 16 matches, Slater emulated Wright's 1952 feat of being named the Football Writers Association's Player of the Year. Team-mate Flowers, Blackburn's Ronnie Clayton and Hibernian's Joe Baker had been strongly tipped as well but the vote went to Slater 12 months after another Cup final centre-half, Luton's Syd Owen, had walked away with the prize.

It was the crowning glory of his playing days, although the presentation of the OBE in 1982 was to be a bigger thrill still.

Another triumph, another toast . . . Wolves' players lap up their First Division championship triumph after their victory over Tottenham Hotspur at Molineux in 1954. From left: Jimmy Mullen, Bill Shorthouse, Bert Williams, Billy Wright, Dennis Wilshaw, Eddie Stuart, Peter Broadbent, Ron Flowers, Johnny Hancocks, Roy Swinbourne, Bill Slater.

Slater was to play another 85 games for Wolves — a club slipping into decline in the early 1960s — before being rewarded for 11 years of magnificent service with a free transfer in the summer of 1963.

Then 36 and shortly to graduate as a Bachelor of Science, he was on the verge of taking up the post as deputy director of the new Crystal Palace Sports Centre. With great regret, he decided it would be impossible for him to continue playing for Wolves. Before departing for a second brief spell at Brentford prior to retirement, though, he was given a memorable send-off. At the end of his last home game — a 2-0 victory over Blackpool — the crowd gave him a standing ovation and the players of both sides ensured he made a worthy exit by lining the route back to the dressing-room.

Cullis had his say at a special 1963 dinner in the player's honour at Wolverhampton's Victoria Hospital, where he said: 'I know of no-one who created a greater impact on the players at Molineux than Bill — with his self-discipline, good behaviour and sportsmanship. I wish we had many more like him.'

Slater's football career had taken him over distant horizons and to many corners of the world. But his life outside the game was flourishing as well and he hardly gave a second thought to the speculation linking him with the jobs of top F.A. coach and even England manager. In 1964, he left Crystal Palace and became director of physical education at Liverpool University. Six years later, he was back at Birmingham as head of the physical education department, then he furthered his involvement with the National Sports Council by becoming a paid officer in 1984.

In football and out of it, he was a success in every sense of the word.

FULL INTERNATIONAL CAPS (12)

(England score given first)

1954: Wales (Wembley) 3-2; West Germany (Wembley) 3-1.

1958: Scotland (Hampden) 4-0; Portugal (Wembley) 2-1; Yugoslavia (Belgrade) 0-5; USSR (Moscow) 1-1; USSR (Gothenburg) 2-2; Brazil (Gothenburg) 0-0; Austria (Boras) 2-2; USSR (Gothenburg) 0-1; USSR (Wembley) 5-0.

1960: Scotland (Hampden) 1-1.

WOLVES APPEARANCES

League: 310. F.A. Cup: 23. European: 6. Total: 339. Goals: 25.

CHAPTER 10

John Richards

IT'S ONE OF FOOTBALL'S GREAT INJUSTICES THAT John Richards — the most prolific marksman in Wolverhampton Wanderers' history — won only one full cap for England. And it's no exaggeration to say he could easily have won 20 or 30 had he been born 15 years or so later, although a certain Steve Bull might have had something to say about that!

Richards possessed the sort of goal-scoring record that might well have made him the country's No. 9 for several seasons. But England's good fortune in having so many renowned strikers was his misfortune. He played against Northern Ireland in the 1973 Home Internationals and was named in the senior squad on several other occasions. But he never kicked another ball at that level, confined to the shadows by men like Allan Clarke, Geoff Hurst, Martin Chivers, Mike Channon, Joe Royle, Malcolm Macdonald and Frank Worthington.

The other big threat to Richards' prospects was injury — an occupational hazard that played an increasing part as his career progressed. But, it seemed, no amount of knee surgery could dull his appetite for goals and he repeatedly bounced back to finally take his place proudly as the club's all-time leading scorer.

To Wolves fans, he was King John. To his team-mates and

those others fortunate enough to know him, he was the model professional. Dedicated, unassuming, honest and Mr Nice Guy. In other words, very, very popular. If there were a dozen more like him around today to influence the next generation of hopefuls, football wouldn't be the troubled game it is.

The story started 70 miles or so North of Wolverhampton in the Cheshire town of Warrington, where he was born on November 11, 1950. He played rugby league, as well as soccer, at school, appearing in the same town teams in both sports as Steve Kindon, one of his Molineux colleagues of a decade later.

While making progress down the academic road that was to lead to six O levels and one A level, Richards was promoted to the Lancashire Grammar Schools team — and started to impress the talent-hunters. In 1969, at 18, he scored six goals against the English Public Schools side in a tournament at the Butlin's Holiday Camp, Bognor Regis. Then he went on to hit two more in a 3-1 win against the Arsenal youth side.

Among the people to bid him hi-de-hi was Tony Penman, a Midlands-based Wolves scout who quickly alerted those in power at Molineux. The Richards family home was almost exactly half-way between the football hotbeds of Merseyside and Manchester, so any outsiders had to move quickly if they were to be the lucky ones in capitalising on his late entry into professional football.

A few days after returning from the Sussex resort, Richards received a visit from chief scout Joe Gardiner, himself a former Wolves player. Gardiner beat his rivals from Sheffield Wednesday and Derby County by about two days in offering the teenager a trial, which came in the form of a 4-0 reserve win at home to Derby County in Wolves' last Central League game of 1968-69.

'I didn't score,' Richards recalls, 'but, when we were getting changed afterwards, a little fellow came in and said: "Well done, son. How would you like to sign for us?" When he went out, I turned and asked Jimmy Seal, who had just scored a hat-trick, who the gentleman was. He said it was the club chairman, John Ireland!

Picking up the pieces . . . a simple tap-in at Arsenal with Bob Wilson and Peter Simpson grounded and Frank McLintock helpless.

'I went down to Molineux on the following Sunday morning to sign and remember how impressed I was by all the trophies in the cabinet in the foyer. Wolverhampton Wanderers were still one of the biggest clubs in the country and I found the place very awe-inspiring. I went in to see Bill McGarry, the manager, and remember sipping a cup of coffee and getting all the skin down my chin. That's how nervous I was! I was shaking like a leaf. We agreed a contract of £20 a week and I went into digs with a Mrs Eagle in Bradmore, where Barry Powell was already in residence. Unfortunately, I had already booked a holiday for the August and was a bit apprehensive about telling Bill I wanted a week or two off at a time when footballers are generally grafting away after the summer!

'But he let me go and, when I came back, I belatedly set about proving I had the necessary commitment to make it in the game. I played in the reserves, scored all five goals in one game at Blackburn in the November and felt incredibly proud at being on the books. I used to get off the bus near the ground and dawdle to the door, hoping people would see me and say: "Oh, look, there's a Wolves player!" I laugh now but my only ambition was to play ONE game in the first team. That's all! Just to be able to say I had played for Wolves.'

Richards' modest goal was reached rather sooner than he expected because McGarry pulled him to one side in training on Friday, February 27, 1970, and told him he was playing in the following day's derby at Albion. He didn't score but did enough in a 3-3 draw to retain his place for the next three games of a campaign in which Wolves finished 13th after failing to win any of their last 13 League matches.

Then came an end-of-season venture in the often ill-fated Anglo-Italian Cup, in which the youngster scored his first first-team goal and learned another harsh reality of life as a professional footballer.

'We had won both of our home games against Fiorentina and Lazio and arrived in Italy the following week three or four days before our first away match,' he added. 'That meant there was no curfew for a couple of nights and, after a few of us had been down to the local pizzeria, I found myself having a drink of sherry with my room-mate, Bertie Lutton. I would like to know what happened for the rest of the evening because the next thing I could remember was the coach, Sammy Chung, banging on our door next morning and telling us we were due out for training.

'I must have got into a bit of a state because I woke up with a dreadful headache. We dressed as quickly as we could and sprinted towards the coach waiting to take us to the training ground. But the combination of the hangover, the bright sun and the hotel's white marble floor played a few tricks when we rushed into the reception area. We negotiated the doors all right but just didn't see the steps outside and both went flying down them head first. Unlike the players, Bill

Typically Richards . . . a sight Wolves fans came to know so well and love. A right-foot shot, a stranded keeper and another goal, this time the decider in a 2-1 win against Liverpool in 1972-73.

McGarry didn't say a word when we got aboard. He made his point, though, when training started and had the two of us in the goalmouth for about 20 minutes, heading crosses drilled in from both wings. That just made our headaches worse and taught us to be very moderate about having a drink in future!'

Richards, who also toured Zambia and Malawi with Wolves youths in his early months at Molineux, recovered sufficiently to score in the 3-1 victory in Fiorentina. But defeat in a bruising battle against Lazio ended the club's interest in the competition.

It was back to the reserves at the start of 1970-71 and, with Wolves steaming on towards UEFA Cup qualification via a final League placing of fourth, Richards had to be content with a mere handful of appearances in the starting line-up. But he had a dozen other outings as sub and, in that role, scored in a home League win over Huddersfield Town and in an F.A. Cup fourth-round defeat at Derby. There was also the satisfaction of playing a small part in bringing a cup to Molineux — albeit only the Texaco Cup.

'My first League goal was obviously an important milestone,' Richards says. 'Jimmy McCalliog took a corner on the right at the South Bank End and I finished it off with a left-foot volley at the far post. But there was only one other goal that season and it wasn't until 1971-72 that I really made my breakthrough. Hugh Curran and Bobby Gould were moving on and I went in alongside Derek Dougan early in the season.

'I played about 35 League matches, scored 13 goals and it all came together. On top of that, we had a great run to the UEFA Cup final and scored goals everywhere we went. The fashion in those days was for teams playing away in the first leg to defend. But we did the opposite — through a combination of naivety and the fact we had an attacking side. We treated it as a big adventure which was there to be enjoyed.

'We scored four against Academica Coimbra in Portugal, then three in Holland against Den Haag. I got the only goal in the snow in Carl Zeiss Jena and we were delighted to hang on for a draw away to Juventus in the quarter-final. After that game, we overheard one of the Italians say: 'That's it.' He knew that if his side didn't win their home leg, they were in trouble, especially if they conceded a goal at home in the process. We edged through in the second leg and then did the same against Ferencvaros after drawing in Hungary.

'The big disappointment was that we were up against Tottenham in the final. Playing another English side was an anti-climax and there wasn't that much interest considering it was a European final. We lost 2-1 at home and drew 1-1 away but it had still been a great experience.'

Richards was not the target-man type of forward, although his excellent close control made him an ideal holder-up of the ball. His real strengths were his razor-sharp reactions around the penalty area, his quick turns, his eye for a ball to run on to and, of course, his precious ability to put it in the net. Many of his goals were from long clearances, flicked on by

Head-master . . . nodding past Manchester United's Jimmy Nichol for a goal in the Old Trafford rain in May, 1979.

Dougan, the characteristic finish being a hard, low right-foot shot.

They were attributes that began to attract a wider circle of admirers. In 1971-72, he added to his England Grammar School honours by being selected for the England under-23 tour to East Germany, Poland and Russia. And, typically, he marked the call-up with a goal, scoring against the Poles despite having broken his hand in the German game.

As if that trip wasn't enough on top of a season of 46 club games, Richards also took part in the first leg of Wolves' summer tour of America and New Zealand. But he was making such great strides that he couldn't really get too much football. And any tiredness he may have felt was right out of his system by the time Wolves kicked off their 1972-73 campaign — a season of immense personal satisfaction.

Richards rattled in 27 League goals, three in the F.A. Cup, three in the League Cup and three in the Texaco Cup. They were figures that confirmed all his young promise. His scoring success also had three direct spin-offs, Wolves managing a final fifth place in the First Division, reaching two cup semi-finals and their runaway top-scorer elevating himself to the full England team.

The call from Sir Alf Ramsey came for the visit of Northern Ireland on May 12, 1973 — a game switched from Belfast to Goodison Park because of the political problems across the water. That caused a nostalgic coincidence in the life of the eager debutant, who recalls: 'We stayed at the Lord Daresbury Hotel in Warrington, about six miles from where I used to live. And we trained on a pitch I had played on many times as a lad! I was certainly in familiar surroundings but it was still a shock when I was told I was actually playing. We had three front men — Chivers, Channon and me — so I had to play on the left. I didn't mind that in itself but I didn't have a very good game. We won 2-1 but it all passed me by and I should have imposed myself more on things. I was a bit overawed and didn't show enough initiative.

'I wasn't even sub when Allan Clarke returned for the next two games against Wales and Scotland at Wembley and, although I also went on the unhappy trip to Poland that cost us our place in the 1974 World Cup finals, I didn't figure in that game, nor in the ones in Czechoslovakia, Russia and Italy on the same tour.'

Whatever his disappointment at not establishing himself in the England team, the domestic 1972-73 season had been one of success for player and club alike. He scored his first two first-team hat-tricks — at home to Stoke City and Everton — and Wolves qualified again for Europe through their League placing. They also enjoyed tremendous runs in the two cups, falling in the League Cup to their UEFA Cup conquerors Tottenham, this time in a two-legged semi-final. In the F.A. Cup, Manchester United and Coventry City were among their victims before they slipped 1-0 against Leeds United at the last-four stage.

'It was a case of so near yet so far,' he added. 'The club

Snowball . . . slogging it out with Stoke City's Mike Doyle.

hadn't been to Wembley for 13 years and I remember looking round the dressing-room after the second defeat and seeing the disappointed looks on the faces of Mike Bailey, Frank Munro and Dave Wagstaffe — older players who had given Wolves years of excellent service. It wasn't too bad for me being young but they obviously wondered whether they would ever get to Wembley. Happily, we all finally made it in 1973-74.'

Richards, married in 1973, actually had a poor League season, failing to score in any of the opening ten First Division games and, all told, managing only nine goals in 26 League appearances. But he hit a purple patch with seven in seven League Cup appearances and, with one apiece in the F.A. Cup and UEFA Cup, totalled a respectable 18. It was also the season, however, in which he suffered the start of the injury problems which dogged the rest of his career and at times threatened it.

Early in the campaign, though, an absence of a different kind was thrust on him when he was sent off for retaliation after scoring in the first leg of the UEFA Cup first-round tie against Belenenses in Portugal. That hot-headedness left him suspended both for the second leg and for the second round, in which Wolves went out to East Germans Locomotiv Leipzig on the away goals rule.

A fine run of 16 goals in 21 games in mid-winter brought his season to life, the last two of them crucial efforts in the two-leg League Cup semi-final against Norwich City in late January. 'We played really well at Carrow Road in the first leg and were unlucky only to draw 1-1,' he says. 'I can still remember us arriving back at the hotel afterwards and noticing how quiet Bill McGarry was. He knew we should have sewn it up that night and was obviously worried that we were going to go out in another semi-final.

'But we edged through 1-0 in a very close second leg. I scored the winner after the Doog flicked on a long kick by Phil Parkes. I headed it past David Stringer and set off on my own towards goal at the North Bank End. I had so much time to think about it and finally just hammered my shot hard and low under Kevin Keelan. It was the most memorable goal I ever scored because it got us over that semi-final barrier and actually got us to Wembley. That's what really mattered.'

After averaging a goal a game on the road to the final, Richards nearly missed the big day itself against Manchester City on March 2. He had been carrying a pelvic injury for several weeks and sat out three of the previous four League games. Even when finally given the go-ahead for Wembley during the squad's seaside build-up at Worthing, fears of him aggravating the injury meant he spent the Friday night wearing a corset and with his ankles and knees strapped together!

Everything turned out happily on the day, though — but only just. 'I felt another recurrence when I stretched for a Geoff Palmer cross in the first half,' Richards recalls. 'But, fortunately, I missed the ball and Kenny Hibbitt followed up to put us in front. Then, the boss had Barry Powell warming up as sub in the second half and I assumed I was to be taken off. But Dave Wagstaffe pulled a muscle in the meantime and he went

Air-play . . . Richards loses out to David O'Leary and Wolves lose out to Arsenal. F.A. Cup semi-final flop, Villa Park, 1979.

off instead. A few minutes later, Alan Sunderland's cross deflected off Rodney Marsh's heel and I scored the winner. Things could have been so different!'

Wolves' 2-1 victory, joyously acclaimed by the masses who had splashed out all of 80p for their terrace tickets, was also due in no small part to keeper Gary Pierce, who stepped in for the injured Parkes and produced a man-of-the-match performance. And Richards' personal delight at three memorable seasons was compounded when wife Pam presented him with their first daughter in that same year.

Another two England under-23 caps had also come his way and he remained in contention for a senior place. But, for the first time since 1929-30, Wolves didn't have anyone selected for a full international. And Richards, who wasn't fit to play again that season after Wembley, was, sadly and somewhat mysteriously, overlooked by England for the rest of his career. The closest he went to a second senior appearance was in a game or two as an unused sub. But the big breakthrough eluded him.

His claims were never as strong in 1974-75, for, in a year of change marked by the demise of Dougan, he totalled only 15 goals. Wolves went out of the F.A. Cup, the League Cup and the UEFA Cup at the first hurdles and Richards found himself with a variety of attacking partners including Sunderland, Kindon, John Farley and Peter Withe.

A satisfactory 12th place was the outcome to Wolves' League efforts and few would have predicted that relegation was just around the corner in 1975-76. Wolves still had an abundance of talent in their squad, as proven by their journey to the final of the F.A. Youth Cup, to the fourth round of the League Cup and to the quarter-final of the F.A. Cup. In the latter competition, they finally fell in a home replay against Manchester United after accounting for Arsenal, Ipswich Town and Charlton Athletic.

The 3-0 Molineux victory over Charlton on Valentine's Day brought Richards an unlikely hat-trick as substitute and he reeled off another treble when visiting Newcastle United were crushed 5-0 two months later. With 25 League and cup goals, it was a good season for Richards amid a poor one for the club. They never recovered from a bad start and became the latest victims of the 'We're too good to go down' myth.

McGarry paid the ultimate price by being sacked in favour of Chung — and Richards was having problems of his own. He had some foreign bodies removed from the back of his knee in the summer of 1976 and was to become all-too-familiar with the route to and from both the operating theatre and the various specialists.

'All my problems started when we went away to Southport

Same faces, different colours . . . Richards in combat with Asa Hartford in a match against the Scottish League North of the border in 1972-73. It was his only appearance for the Football League.

for a few days in between a League game at Everton and the F.A. Cup quarter-final at Manchester United in early March,' he says. 'We were training in a park and I jarred my knee going over in a little pothole. It swelled up for a couple of days, went down again and then got worse towards the end of the season. I had it X-rayed and went in for surgery in the close season.

'Then, after we'd reported back at the start of 1976-77, I collided with Gary Pierce in training at Molineux and I was back in hospital. This time it was a cartilage operation and I didn't play my first match in the Second Division until the end of November.'

By then, Wolves were well on the way to what proved to be a title-winning season, Richards belatedly playing a full part with 20 League and cup goals. He hit a hat-trick at Orient in his second comeback game, scored two at home to Plymouth Argyle a week later and completed a magnificent burst of seven goals in three games with a brace in the 3-3 draw at Chelsea. Although Munro remained team captain, Richards was appointed club skipper in February, a few weeks before the club clinched promotion at Plymouth and then the championship at home to Chelsea.

It had been a very comfortable return to the First Division but life was, predictably, more difficult in the top flight. Wolves finished strongly to survive in 15th place, Richards managing only a modest 13 goals (including a Molineux hat-trick against Leicester City) despite emerging as an almost ever-present. His right knee had not regained its previous strength and there were again fears over his fitness when the 1978-79 campaign got under way. He played in the early-season games against Leeds and Bristol City — but didn't reappear until the end of February.

Another round of X-rays, consultations and visits to specialists began and this time it looked like being the end. 'It was the make-or-break really,' Richards said. 'Osteo-arthritis had set in and the specialists strongly recommended that I considered quitting. I had had problems for three years and it was an understandable reaction. But I decided to have another operation. If they had found nothing, my career would have been over because there would have been nowhere else to turn. But they found a small piece of cartilage and a piece of soft tissue which had stuck in the joint.

'From that moment, I was confident I would play again,

although it was a long slog for fitness. I spent many hours on the perimeter track at Molineux and it was a session there that gave me one of my most humorous memories. Dr. Horsley, the club doctor, was standing in the tunnel watching as I ran in front of the North Bank and down the Waterloo Road side. As I and the physio, Kevin Walters, neared the corner of the South Bank, I became aware we were being joined by someone else. I turned round and there was the doc, galloping behind us in his suit and carrying his medical bag as he monitored my progress!'

At the front line, Chung had been replaced as manager by John Barnwell after another dismal start. But the season was well into its second half when Richards made his long-awaited return. 'It was for the game at Arsenal on February 24 and I assumed I would be sub,' he added. 'When we arrived at Highbury just after 2 p.m., Barney asked me to pop out and move his car. That seemed to confirm I wasn't playing. But I was just making my way back in through the famous marble halls when the gaffer told me I was playing. I was amazed!'

As befitted Richards on these occasions, he scored the winner — and modestly accepts it was his nine goals in 17 League outings that spelled the difference between survival and relegation. He also played in the latter stages of the club's journey to the last four of the F.A. Cup, helping eliminate Crystal Palace and Shrewsbury Town before the semi-final jinx struck again in a dreadful 2-0 defeat against Arsenal at Villa Park.

For the player himself, it had been a crucial year which he had come through in such style as to be offered a six-year contract several months later. And despite reported interest from other clubs, Richards pledged the rest of his football life to Molineux. On the club's part, it was an astonishing gamble to take on an injury-plagued player. But no-one could accuse them of small-mindedness at the time. The controversial new John Ireland Stand had recently gone up, Emlyn Hughes had been prised away from the security of Anfield and Wolves also splashed out a sensational £1,469,000 to bring Aston Villa and Scotland striker Andy Gray to Molineux.

The Gray-Richards partnership immediately struck gold, both netting in high-scoring victories over Everton and Manchester United in their first two games in unison. Wolves were revitalised, destined to finish sixth in the First Division, although the goals at times dried up and Richards suffered the indignity of being sent off in England (against Villa) for the only time. The club also went back to Wembley and won the League Cup for a second time, this time at the expense of Nottingham Forest, Richards ending an eventful season in the upper teens to overshadow his partner's 15 goals.

'This was the second time in my career that I felt Wolves were on the brink of becoming one of the country's top clubs,' Richards added. 'The other was in the 1972-74 period and it's strange that, each time, we won the League Cup the year after losing an F.A. Cup semi-final and two years before we were relegated. I also scored the goal that took us to Wembley both times.

'In 1980, that was in a two-leg semi-final against Swindon Town. We lost 2-1 away in the first leg and were struggling a bit to break them down at Molineux in what was my 350th game for the club. Then we got cracking and I scored two and Mel Eves one. In the final, we were underdogs because Forest had won the cup for the previous two years and were considered by many to be the best team in England. But we defended superbly and Andy tapped in the winner in the second half. But I must admit it was a poor game. Next day, there must have been almost 100,000 lining the streets of Wolverhampton when we came back and, once again, we were made to realise just how important the football club are to the town.

'I shared a room with Andy on the overnight trips and we had some laughs. When we first arrived at hotels, we would race not for the bed by the window or for the bottle opener, but for the ice bucket! He'd had knee problems like me and many's the time we used to be sitting with our ice-packs in our room on

Pick of the bunch . . . Richards beats Manchester City defenders Mike Doyle and Tommy Booth with the shot that brought the League Cup to Molineux for the first time — his most famous goal.

Friday nights, trying to get rid of swelling. And that's just how we spent the evening before the Forest final!'

Another trophy in the cabinet or not, Wolves were on the slippery slope. The promise wasn't maintained in 1980-81 and Wolves — well served by 17 goals from Richards — finished 18th for the second time in three years. They went out of the UEFA Cup in the first round against PSV Eindhoven and, once again, compensation came in knockout competition closer to home.

This time it was with a run to the F.A. Cup semi-final thanks to victories over Stoke City, Watford, Wrexham and Middlesbrough. Bogey side Tottenham were their opponents in the last four at Hillsborough, where Wolves failed to make the most of a helping hand from referee Clive Thomas. He awarded them a dubious last-gasp penalty from which Willie Carr took the tie to a replay at Highbury but Wolves never got out of the starting blocks second time around and crashed 3-0 to the eventual winners. It was a third taste of F.A. Cup semi-final heartbreak for Richards, Derek Parkin, John McAlle and Kenny Hibbitt.

But the gloom was even greater when Wolves were

relegated in 1981-82, the season Barnwell was sacked and replaced by Ian Greaves. Richards had overtaken Billy Hartill (170), Johnny Hancocks (168) and Jimmy Murray (166) as the club's all-time top scorer but the end was nigh, Barnwell unsuccessfully trying to unload him as bait in a 1981 exchange deal for Birmingham defender Joe Gallagher.

Although he went on to make 33 first-team outings that season, Richards — still club captain — scored only four times. His 350th League appearance for the club (at Middlesbrough) was quickly followed by relegation and the shock of Wolves going into liquidation for the first time. Richards' time was almost up. He made a paltry four appearances in the stuttering 1982-83 promotion season and at one stage became so disenchanted with life in the reserves that he emerged from his 'perfect club man' image to moan: 'The Christians had a better chance with the Romans than I've had at Molineux this season!'

It was sad and ironic that Dougan was now chairman of the crumbling club his old attacking colleague had fallen out with. Richards had two enjoyable months on loan to Derby and was given a free transfer at the end of 1982-83, moving on to spend two pleasant years in the Madeira sunshine with Portuguese second division club Maritimo. He returned for an emotional farewell in a second testimonial game in 1985 and, now, a father of two daughters, is happily employed in the leisure services department of Wolverhampton Council.

As well as his one full England cap, his six under-23 and two under-21 caps, the former Midland Footballer of the Year and national Young Player of the Year also played three times for England B — on a 1977-78 tour of Singapore, New Zealand and Malaysia — and once for the Football League. He never played in a losing England team at any level. Richards is also Wolves' top scorer in the F.A. Cup and League Cup, though only fourth behind Hartill, Hancocks and Murray in their League list.

Asking him to choose his favourite goal is like asking Paul

McCartney to select his best piece of music or Dustin Hoffman his best film role. But he says: 'I'll plump for the first of my three against Everton in 1973. Derek Parkin crossed from the left, I knocked the ball to my left near the edge of the area and then smashed it left-footed on the up past Gordon West and into the far corner. I'm quite happy for those great Wolves fans to remember me for moments like that!'

FULL INTERNATIONAL CAPS (1)

(England score given first)

1973: Northern Ireland (Everton) 2-1.

WOLVES APPEARANCES

League: 385. F.A. Cup: 44. League Cup: 33. European: 14. Others: 10. Total: 486. Goals: 194.

CHAPTER 11

Steve Bull

HE HASN'T KICKED A BALL FOR WOLVERhampton Wanderers in the First Division and he was playing in the West Midlands League just over five years ago. His rough edges at times bear out his comparatively recent non-League past and there are those only too eager to place a question mark against his suitability for international football. But his sheer volume of goals have done his talking for him and ensured his place for ever in the Molineux hall of fame.

Steve Bull rates alongside the Richardses, the Swinbournes, the Wilshaws and the Westcotts, simply because he has done everything — and a lot more — he could possibly have done on the stage on which Wolves have so far given him the chance to perform. His predecessors did their stuff in the First Division and, in some cases, in Europe. Bull has had to do it in more modest company so far but he has done it magnificently.

In 1987-88, he scored 52 club goals — a fantastic achievement even in the Fourth Division. The following season in the Third, he made further breathtaking strides with another 50. On top of that, he has achieved the difficult feat of breaking into the international limelight from the lower divisions, first as an over-age player in the England under-21s, then as a B international and, finally, as a fully-fledged member of Bobby Robson's senior side.

Game for a laugh . . . Mark Kendall, Steve Bull and Andy Mutch celebrate promotion from the Fourth Division in the dressing-room of Newport County's Somerton Park ground in April, 1988.

The roller-coaster of success slowed down slightly during Wolves' season of Second Division consolidation in 1989-90. But he still rattled in the 27 League and cup goals that left his passport to Italy for the World Cup finals signed, sealed and delivered.

Bull's story, as well as being an inspiration to every young man hoping to make his way in the game, is football's most remarkable of recent years. Where it will end, nobody knows. But no one man has made a bigger impact in the British game in the last four years, nor played a bigger part in lifting the spirits of the thousands who see Molineux as their second home.

In Wolverhampton and various other parts of the Black Country, Stephen George Bull is a cult figure. A superstar on whose every goal and every movement they hang. In these times of hero worship, he's the ideal hero — down-to-earth, modest and totally unspoilt by his success.

I had the pleasure of being the first journalist summoned to Molineux when he and his best mate, Andy Thompson, made the move from neighbouring West Bromwich Albion on November 20, 1986. I've also had the pleasure of spending many hours in his company since and, apart from the change of hairstyle to distinctive crew cut and the sporting of an occasional suntan from his overseas trips, there has been no change. He's just the same young man who quietly sipped coffee in the boardroom after completing the out-of-the-blue move that revived his fledgling career.

At the time, I wondered how two players from the fringe of an unattractive Albion side could possibly solve the many massive problems confronting new Wolves manager Graham Turner. Wolves were in the middle of the Fourth Division at the time, had just been held to two 1-1 draws by Chorley in the first round of the F.A. Cup and were sweating on an F.A. backlash to the riot staged by some of their followers at Torquay earlier in the month.

Thompson, picked up for £32,000, and Bull, in hindsight a £64,000 'steal', were immediately pencilled in for their Wolves debuts in the Saturday home game with Wrexham. It would be no exaggeration to say they were less than conspicuous. Wolves, watched by only 5,252 and probably jeered by half of them, were hammered 3-0 and, of the newcomers' contribution, the *Express & Star* comment was: 'It was no day for the two debutants to shine. But Bull should prove a useful muscular ally in time to Andy Mutch.'

Things were to get a lot worse before they got even a bit better. Two days later, Wolves headed up the M6 in an effort to resolve their unexpectedly awkward cup confrontation with Chorley. It was resolved all right — 3-0 in favour of the humble Multipart League side at neutral Bolton. The cup-tied Bull and Thompson had watched disbelievingly from the stand as Wolves suffered the worst night in their proud history. Worse than that, many thought they had just witnessed the last rites being administered to a club repeatedly at death's door in previous years.

'I have to admit — I wondered what I had let myself in for

Steve Bull, Wolverhampton Wanderers and England.

when I saw that game,' Bull said. 'It was embarrassing for everybody connected with the club and the fans made their feelings quite clear. It wasn't the happiest journey home we've ever had!'

Bull was back for the League game at Lincoln five days later but it made no difference, Wolves losing their way in the second-half fog and crashing to their third successive 3-0 defeat. The club who had won the title three times and the F.A. Cup twice in the previous 40 years, were struggling in the

Fourth Division and looking anxiously over their shoulders as the dark shadow of relegation for the fourth consecutive season lengthened.

But, slowly, the tide began to turn. Bull's 75th-minute shot on a cold December night in South Wales gave him his first Wolves goal and his side an unconvincing 1-0 victory over Cardiff City in the preliminary round of the Freight Rover Trophy. And he struck again with an opportunist effort to secure three useful points at Hartlepool in the following game.

When Bull rattled in two more in an exciting 4-3 Freight Rover flourish at home to Bournemouth, fans were beginning to think Turner's investment might have been a good idea after all in contrast to the host of non-descripts the club had signed in the previous two or three seasons. Bull's touch certainly left a lot to be desired and he looked at times like a fish out of water — or even a Bull in a china shop. But he knew where the goal was.

Christmas came and went with another couple of goals from the newcomer despite another downturn in results. Then a Bull-inspired 2-0 League win at Cardiff provided another false start because, when Hereford United and Crewe Alexandra won at Molineux in the next seven days, Wolves were back to square one.

Stockport County looked like piling on the agony when they provided the opposition on another dismal Molineux afternoon on February 7, 1987. They pinched the lead just after half-time in a dreadful game and looked like becoming the 11th away side to win at the ground in less than six months. Then, to the joy of a 3,238 crowd, a very strange thing happened. Thompson, Bull and Micky Holmes plundered goals in the last 14 minutes and Wolves had recorded an unexpected victory.

Although Bull's name was surprisingly absent from the list of marksmen in the next two games, the side suddenly discovered how to score again, hammering in a total of eight in crushing Burnley away and Aldershot at home. And, shortly

Champions again . . . Bull, Gary Bellamy and Phil Robinson on Wolves' lap of honour after they clinched the Third Division title against Sheffield United in May, 1989.

after useful draws against two of the clubs destined for promotion, Northampton Town and Preston North End, they embarked on the run that was to confirm they were well and truly on the way back.

Starting at home to Swansea City on March 14, they reeled off eight victories on the trot for only the third time in their history and, after a costly Friday night slip at promotion rivals Southend United, bounced back with four more wins in a row.

It was during that second spell of success that Bull really burst into the limelight, scoring twice at home to Lincoln, once at Exeter City two days later and then three in the last League game of the season, at home to Hartlepool. It was the first hat-trick by a Wolves player for nearly a decade and, although it wasn't quite enough to secure automatic promotion, it made the club hot favourites to go up via the newly-introduced play-offs.

Third Division football seemed just round the corner when Colchester United were brushed aside 2-0 on aggregate in the play-off semi-final — Bull hitting his 19th Wolves goal of the season to add to the three he had scored for Albion in the autumn — but Aldershot defied all the odds by handing out a 3-0 beating over two legs in the final.

'We couldn't believe we had missed promotion after going so close,' Bull added. 'We had proved ourselves to be the best side in the Fourth Division over the previous three or four months and it seemed unfair that we had lost out to Aldershot, who had finished two places and nine points behind us in the League table. But they were the new rules and we just had to put up with them and set about going up automatically the following season.'

That Wolves did, overcoming an uneasy start during which several hundred of their followers brought shameful scenes to the seaside town of Scarborough on kick-off day. There, Bull, inevitably, scored his side's first goal of the season and, in fact, failed to find the net in only three of the first 14 League matches.

The Tipton Terrier had 16 goals to his credit by the end of October but it was while he was suspended for a harsh sending-off at home to Tranmere Rovers that Wolves went top of the Fourth Division for the first time. It was a position they were to occupy for the rest of the season for all but a few days in mid winter. The rampage of the Bull continued as non-League

Fifty up . . . Bull turns to celebrate his 50th and last club goal of 1988-89, this one against Sheffield United in the title decider.

Cheltenham Town suffered his second Molineux hat-trick but there was a warning from Turner to curb his admirable enthusiasm and aggression after the victory at Colchester had been marred by his second dismissal in just over a month.

As well as giving the South Bank masses the sort of goal-scoring hero they had been denied since the departure of John Richards and Andy Gray, Bull was giving rival managers something to think about and both Chelsea and Wimbledon made overtures about signing him. But the modest 22-year-old merely said: 'I love Wolves and I love the West Midlands. All I want to do is carry on scoring the goals that will get us out of the Fourth Division and, hopefully, higher still.

'I know I must work hard to convert a higher percentage of the chances I get but I have always thought I could score goals. It's just that I wasn't really given the opportunity at

Albion. Here, I seem to be getting through Fourth Division defences a lot and the goals are there to be had.'

Bull was already head and shoulders above everybody else in the country's goalscoring lists and had 24 to his name by the turn of the year. Wolves already looked certs to go up but another exciting target — Wembley — appeared on their horizon as they overcome Swansea and Bristol City in the Freight Rover Trophy. The competition was renamed the Sherpa Van Trophy in mid-season but it made no difference to Bull as he blitzed Third Division Brentford with his second hat-trick of the season and then squelched through the Exeter mud to provide a repeat performance.

It was clear that history was in the making, for Bull was storming towards Dennis Westcott's all-time club record of 43 League and cup goals in a season, set in 1938-39. Helped by the 46-match League programme and the multitude of cup-ties Wolves were involved in, Bull was well on course for 50 — and crashed in yet another hat-trick this time at home to Darlington on March 26. And he finally overhauled the 1930s and 1940s hero's tally by scoring both goals in a 2-0 Easter Monday triumph over Colchester.

The season still had more than a month to run and Bull put the time to good use by becoming the first man since Peterbrough United's Terry Bly nearly 30 years earlier to score 50 League and cup goals in an English season. He completed his half-century, appropriately enough, on the night Wolves clinched promotion at Newport County, and netted another two as the side beat Hartlepool to lift the Fourth Division title and so become the first club ever to win the championships of all four divisions.

Bull, whose only real disappointment was that he failed to score at Wembley when the club also won the Sherpa Van Trophy three weeks later, finished with 52 goals — a staggering haul that will probably never be bettered. But he recalls: 'I never took much notice of the records. They were just something people kept putting in front of me and they would

Same old scenario . . . wheeling away in triumph after a beauty against Oxford United in April, 1990.

tell me again when I had broken them! One day, I'll look back and be proud that I have a place in Wolves history but my only concern was — and still is — just to keep scoring goals.'

Bull suffered a mini-famine at the start of Wolves' 1988-89 Third Division campaign, failing to score in four League games either side of his match-winning brace against Birmingham City in the Littlewoods Cup. But he moved into his stride with four goals in three autumn games and featured in the fireworks as Wolves beat Southend 3-0 on November 5 to go top of the table.

He was now a more complete all-round player, as well as a phenomenal scorer, and Turner was becoming so besieged with unsettling inquiries about his future that he angrily vowed to make no further comment on speculation over the destiny of his prize asset. Surprisingly, Bull had to wait three months for his first hat-trick of the season but, when it came, it revealed an exciting new trait. Not content with merely hitting three goals in a game, he smashed four past Preston on November 26 and four past Port Vale on December 13 before knocking three past Mansfield Town four days later.

It was one of the most extraordinary scoring bursts in Wolves' history, with records and milestones being accomplished almost by the match. His late New Year's Eve equaliser at Brentford was the 100th League and cup goal of his two-club career and, when yet another hat-trick followed at home to Bristol City on January 24, he also completed his Wolves century.

There was simply no end in sight to the fairytale, the lad off the factory floor spearheading Wolves towards a second successive championship triumph and enjoying massive personal glory along the way. His tally of hat-tricks entered double figures when Fulham were sent packing 5-2 and, before he was again the three-goal hero when Bury visited Molineux in March, there was success of a different kind.

For some weeks, Midlands journalists had been banging the international drum on his behalf and it was no surprise when, on February 23, 1989, he was named as an over-age player for England under-21s' game in Albania the following month. Third Division player or not, Bull had simply proved himself too good to be ignored any longer. He didn't score in faraway Tirana but did well enough to keep his place for the return at Ipswich several weeks later — and this time delighted the travelling gold and black army by firing his first international goal.

'It was a great moment,' he recalls. 'It was marvellous just to be representing my country but I was delighted for the Wolves fans, my family and myself when I put that one in. The style of play was different to what I was used to because the ball was played a lot more to my feet, rather than over the top to chase. But I managed to adapt and obviously did enough to warrant another chance.'

Back at Wolves, Bull, remarkably, was threatening to overhaul his 52 club goals of the previous season. After he and

Pompey floored . . . Bull walks all over Portsmouth in Wolves' crushing 5-0 1989 victory at Molineux.

his colleagues had overcome the bitter disappointment of missing out on another Wembley visit in the Sherpa Van Trophy, he stood on 48 goals with three games left after scoring twice against Bristol City on the day Wolves clinched promotion. But his chances of reaching 53 were diminished by his own success. He and Mutch, with whom he had formed a tremendous attacking partnership in the previous two and a half years, were named for the England B team summer tour of Switzerland, Iceland and Norway and were to miss Wolves' final League game — the rearranged fixture at Wigan.

That meant Bull needed five goals in those last three matches and, despite managing one against Northampton and another in the title-clinching draw at home to Sheffield United, the task proved beyond even him. He finished the season with exactly 50 for his club, although his international emergence was to take his club-and-country haul to 54! More imporant, he had to settle for 37 League goals, just one behind Dennis Westcott's club record set in 1946-47.

Bull scored twice on the B tour, once from a penalty in Norway, and, no sooner had he and his girlfriend Julie Dace unpacked his bags, than he received the most exciting news of his life. Bobby Robson, his plans in chaos because of injuries and the long-running title saga involving Liverpool and Arsenal, had rung Wolves secretary Keith Pearson with the message that was to bring more celebrations to Bull and his legions of admirers: he was in the senior England squad for the first time.

Bull, who had proved elusive to contact because of his wish to lie low after his B-team heroics, was up and away again almost immediately, flying to Glasgow Airport and then being chauffeur-driven to link up at Troon with the players preparing for the game against old rivals Scotland at Hampden Park. It was another dream fulfilled but the unassuming striker didn't pay much attention to whether he would actually play or spend an afternoon on the substitutes' bench. The answer, after Robson had passed on a few reassuring words to him en route from the team hotel, was a bit of both — with glorious results.

Bull was duly named among the subs but an injury to Wimbledon's John Fashanu gave him his big chance after only half an hour. The boy from The Lost City had arrived on one of the world's most famous stages, and was later dubbed the Backstreet International. Somehow, it was almost inevitable Bull would mark the occasion in the only way he knew. And so he did.

'It was about ten minutes before the end when it happened,' he says. 'We were leading 1-0 through a goal by Chris Waddle when a cross by Gary Stevens arrived around the edge of the Scottish penalty area. I went up with one of their defenders and the ball bounced down off my shoulder. Nobody else seemed to move, so I just pounced on it and hit it low and hard into the corner of the net. There weren't many England fans there and the ground went so quiet that I wondered whether it had been disallowed. Then I realised the referee was

Czech-mate . . . familiar chaos during another Bull rampage, this time in the England v Czechoslovakia game, April 1990.

heading back towards the centre circle, so I just dropped to my knees. I could have cried.'

As the post-match compliments poured in from renowned ex-strikers like Denis Law and Joe Jordan, Robson called Bull 'the most refreshing player to hit the scene for a very long time.' And, after giving him another international gallop alongside Mutch in an under-21 victory over Poland at Plymouth, he had him back with the senior squad for the end-of-season draw against Denmark in Copenhagen.

Bull again went on as sub, this time less spectacularly, and, with two full caps and another half-century of Wolves goals, had enjoyed another magnificent season. Not only had he contributed an enormous quantity of goals, he had also obliged with some real quality efforts — a tremendous right-foot shot against Mansfield, an overhead volley against Chester City, a stunning left-foot finish at home to Bolton Wanderers and a vital solo effort with the outside of his right foot at Blackpool.

By the end of 1988-89, in astonishingly short time, his 121 Wolves goals had sent him leapfrogging above such famous players as Swinbourne, Wilshaw, Jimmy Mullen, Kenny Hibbitt, Tom Phillipson and Jesse Pye in the club's all-time marksmen list. Only eight players remained ahead of him and three of them — Harry Wood, Westcott and Derek Dougan — were overhauled with the 1989-90 campaign only a few weeks old.

'For the previous two seasons, I had taken money off friends who had bet me I wouldn't score so many goals,' Bull added. 'At the start of our Second Division, my target was 25. Apart from a few games for Albion, I was unknown at that level but I knew I had to keep coming up with the goods to hang on to my England place.'

There weren't the same spectacular sprees as in the previous two or three seasons but Bull remained a prolific scorer nonetheless. He netted twice in the England under-21 game in Poland in the autumn and did likewise for Wolves in successive games against Barnsley and Portsmouth. But the goal that gave his followers the most pleasure was still a week or two away on Sunday, October 15.

It was Bull's first return to West Brom as a player and the script couldn't have been written in a more dramatic fashion, his last-minute goal from Mutch's centre giving Wolves victory. 'I always hoped to go back one day and show Albion what I could do,' he said. 'That game means more than any other to Wolves fans and the thing that pleased me most was that I'd given them something to celebrate. I was lucky enough to do the same in the return game in March and, both times, I think the supporters' heads were in the clouds for days afterwards!'

Bull's form was again attracting the England manager's attention, Robson watching him in action in the midweek game at Leicester City at the start of November. The VIP visit was unbeknown to the player himself, though, which left him all the more dejected after he had tangled with defender Steve Walsh and been shown the red card for the third time. The sickening sequel for Bull was that he learned he had been earmarked for a third full cap at home to Italy later that month — but was now suspended. Instead, he was packed off to Brighton, where he had a lively game in the B international between the two countries the night before the main event.

But Robson promised his chance would come again with the seniors — and it did against Yugoslavia in a 2-1 home win in which he looked as ineffective as in any of his international appearances. He clearly still had some work to do to establish himself in the national side, although the lack of form displayed by his rivals still pointed to him being selected for the World Cup finals.

His Wolves fortunes were no more than steady, either, and he needed a boost to prevent his season becoming one of anti-climax. It came on New Year's Day at Newcastle, where he registered his first hat-trick of the season and then went on to add a fourth goal, all in a stunning second-half onslaught. How fitting it was that he should perform his 'victory roll' goal salute so often that afternoon, for Wolves fans had made history of their own by flying to the North East in a squadron of planes.

There was further statistical significance too. The first two strikes at St. James's Park took Bull's tally of League goals to 100 and the other two made it 100 League goals with Wolves!

The promotion dream continued to flicker throughout the late winter and spring, with Bull — insured by his club in February for £2 million — receiving another Robson visit in late February and obliging with a fine equaliser at home to Watford. It clearly wasn't going to be another 50-goal season but, despite remaining on the bench throughout Brazil's defeat at Wembley, it looked like being an Italian summer.

His superb hat-trick in Wolves' slaughter of Leicester took him past his 25-goal pre-season target and, a fortnight later, he laid his strongest claims yet to a regular England place by scoring two beauties in the 4-2 win over Czechoslovakia — his first goals at Wembley.

'I can't do much more now,' he said. 'I've done my bit

and it's up to the manager to decide whether that's enough to get me on the plane to Italy. I've always looked on going to the World Cup finals as a bonus, although I have to accept I may never have a better chance than this. England may not qualify next time round and, besides, I'll be 29 then and could have picked up a serious injury. You just have to grab success while you can in football.'

Robson gave him something to grab at and something with which to ease his disappointment at Wolves missing promotion, when he finally ended the guessing game and named him in his magical 22 on Monday, May 21 — in between the player winning two more full caps in the home games against Denmark and Uruguay.

So, the boy from the ultimate in working-class backgrounds was on his way to the Greatest Football Show On Earth, where he three times appeared as sub and once featured from the start as England exceeded most expectations by reaching the semi-finals. From Tipton Town to the World Cup finals in five years. An amazing rags-to-riches tale. And, with any luck, it will need updating and rewording in years to come. Unlike the other subjects in this book, a lot of pages in Bull's soccer life story have yet to be written.

FULL INTERNATIONAL CAPS

(11, up to start of 1990-91)

(England score given first)

1989: Scotland (Hampden) 2-0; Denmark (Copenhagen) 1-1; Yugoslavia (Wembley) 2-1.

1990: Czechoslovakia (Wembley) 4-2; Denmark (Wembley) 1-0; Uruguay (Wembley) 1-2; Tunisia (Tunis) 1-1; Eire (Cagliari) 1-1; Holland (Cagliari) 0-0; Egypt (Cagliari) 1-0; Belgium (Bologna) 1-0.

WOLVES APPEARANCES

(Up to start of 1990-91)

League: 161. F.A. Cup: 4. League Cup: 10. Sherpa Van Trophy/Simod Cup: 23. Total: 198. Goals: 148.

Wolverhampton Wanderers Honours

Football League: First Divison champions in 1953-54, 1957-58 and 1958-59; Runners-up in 1937-38, 1938-39, 1949-50, 1954-55 and 1959-60; Second Division champions in 1931-32 and 1976-77; Runners-up in 1966-67 and 1982-83; Third Division champions in 1988-89; Third Division (North) champions in 1923-24; Fourth Division champions in 1987-88.

F.A. Cup: Winners in 1893, 1908, 1949 and 1960; Runners-up in 1889, 1896, 1921 and 1939.

League Cup: Winners in 1973-74 and 1979-80.

Texaco Cup: Winners in 1970-71.

Sherpa Van Trophy: Winners in 1987-88.

European competitions: Played in European Cup in 1958-59 and 1959-60; Played in European Cup Winners' Cup in 1960-61; Played in UEFA Cup in 1971-72 (beaten finalists), 1973-74, 1974-75 and 1980-81.